Guatemala

Guatemala

BY MARION MORRISON

Enchantment of the World
Second Series

Children's Press®

A Division of Scholastic Inc.

NEW YORK TORONTO LONDON AUCKLAND SYDNEY
MEXICO CITY NEW DELHI HONG KONG

Frontispiece: Temple I (the Giant Jaguar) in the Great Plaza at Tikal National Park

Consultant: Patrick Eccles, Outreach Coordinator, Center for Latin American Studies, University of Chicago, Chicago, Illinois

Please note: All statistics are as up-to-date as possible at the time of publication.

Book production by Herman Adler Design

Library of Congress Cataloging-in-Publication Data

Morrison, Marion.
  Guatemala / by Marion Morrison.
       p. cm. — (Enchantment of the world. Second series)
  Includes bibliographical references and index.
  ISBN 0-516-23674-1
  1. Guatemala—Juvenile literature. I. Title. II. Series.
  F1463.2.M67 2005
  972.81—dc22   2005006534

Acknowledgments

Much thanks to Elizabeth Carrillo, Anna McVittie, Canning House London, and the Royal Geographical Society, London.

Cover photo:
Teenage
Guatemalan girl
carries a water pot

Contents

Fruit and vegetable
sellers at a market

Funerary urn from c. A.D. 800–900

A New Start

IN THE DARK, THICK RAIN FOREST OF NORTHERN GUATEMALA, the great Maya city of Tikal lay hidden for centuries. No one knows why these Indians abandoned their magnificent city. But they did, sometime around the year 1000. Gradually, the jungle overtook the pyramids, plazas, and monuments. The ruins were never forgotten entirely; the scattered Indians living in the area must have been aware of them. But the Spaniards who arrived in the sixteenth century showed no interest in ancient Tikal.

Opposite: **A Maya temple in Tikal**

Maya ruins from the ancient city of Tikal

The first real investigation of the Tikal ruins was in 1848 by Modesto Méndez. He was a government official in charge of the Petén, the region where Tikal is located. News of his findings reached Europe. The first European visitor was a Swiss who removed some beautifully carved wooden pieces from a doorway. These pieces are now in a museum in Switzerland. An Englishman, Alfred Percival Maudslay, followed in 1881 and 1882. His men chopped down trees to reveal temples and monuments. Meanwhile, Maudslay sketched, took the first photos of Tikal, and made the first map of the site.

Archaeologist Sylvanus G. Morley of the Carnegie Institution of Washington worked at Tikal for many years early in the twentieth century. He was particularly interested in studying the inscriptions on the monuments. The museum at Tikal is now named after Morley.

Until 1951, when the Guatemalan army built an airstrip, the only way of reaching Tikal was on horseback. Five years later, the Tikal Project was launched by the University of Pennsylvania, working with the Guatemalan government. It was the most comprehensive exploration of a Maya site ever and took more than ten years. Central Tikal covers an area of about 6 square miles (16 square kilometers) and contains some 3,000 separate constructions, including temples, palaces, ball courts, and causeways. More than 100,000 tools, ceremonial objects, pieces of jewelry, and other items have been found there. A million broken pieces of pottery have been collected. In 1970, the Guatemala government created the Tikal

Maya artifacts such as pottery (left) reveal details about that ancient civilization.

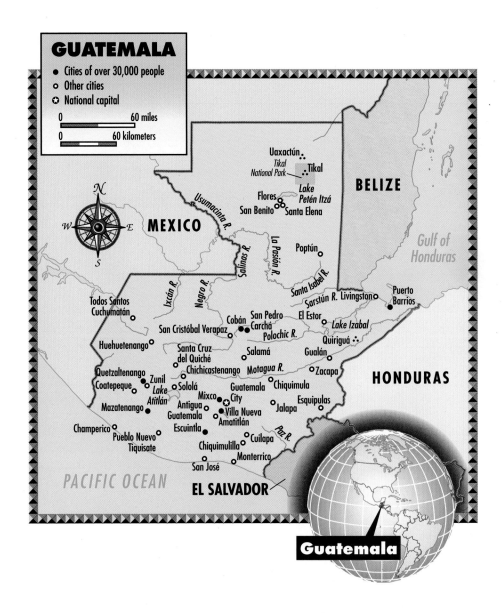

GUATEMALA

- ● Cities of over 30,000 people
- ○ Other cities
- ⊗ National capital

0 ————— 60 miles

0 ————— 60 kilometers

MEXICO

BELIZE

Uaxactún
Tikal National Park — Tikal
Lake Petén Itzá
Flores
San Benito Santa Elena

Usumacinta R.

La Pasión R.

Salinas R.

Ixcán R.

Negro R.

Poptún

Gulf of Honduras

Santa Isabel R.

Sarstún R. Livingston Puerto Barrios

Todos Santos Cuchumatán

Cobán San Pedro El Estor Lake Izabal
San Cristóbal Verapaz Carchá
Polochic R. Quiriguá

Huehuetenango

Santa Cruz del Quiché Salamá Gualán

Quetzaltenango Chichicastenango Motagua R. Zacapa
Coatepeque Zunil Sololá
Lake Atitlán Guatemala City Chiquimula HONDURAS
Mazatenango Antigua Mixco Jalapa Esquipulas
Guatemala Villa Nueva
Escuintla Amatitlán
Champerico Paz R.
Pueblo Nuevo Cuilapa
Tiquisate Chiquimulilla Monterrico
San José Monterrico

PACIFIC OCEAN

EL SALVADOR

Guatemala

National Park Archaeological Project. The site covers 222 square miles (576 sq km). Many ruins in the park have yet to be uncovered.

Visitors who come to Tikal to admire the extraordinary ruins also get a big taste of Guatemala's amazing plant and animal life. The rain forest contains huge trees—including the Maya's sacred tree, the ceiba—as well as lianas, vines, ferns, and a great variety of palms. More than 450 species of birds have been spotted at Tikal. Large bands of spider monkeys can be seen, especially in late afternoon, while deep in the forest large creatures like the jaguar and puma hunt.

A jaguar searches for prey in the rain forest.

Spanish soldiers conquered the Maya tribes in the 1500s. The Spaniards did what most colonizers of the time did—they searched for minerals, farmed, raised cattle, and set about converting the Indians to Christianity. In doing all this, they took the Maya's most prized possession: their land. Much of this land was eventually turned into huge coffee, banana, and sugar plantations.

Besides losing their land, the Maya people have been persecuted by some of the most cruel military regimes the world has seen. In Guatemala, dictatorial governments have worked with wealthy landowners and businessmen to suppress the Maya.

The Maya were colonized by Spanish soldiers.

THE FIRST OF THE RACE.

Any visitor to Guatemala can see, however, that the Maya are a resilient people. Even today, they make up almost half the country's population. They still live in their own communities and manage most of their own affairs. Their markets are busy, and their textiles are the most colorful and superbly woven of any in the Americas. Given that they also live in some of the most scenic parts of Guatemala, including along

A Maya woman sells a variety of colorful textiles.

the magical Lake Atitlán, it is no wonder they are at the center of Guatemala's tourist industry. Artists and writers draw on Maya legend for inspiration, while Maya Nobel Peace Prize winner Rigoberta Menchú Tum has devoted her life to fighting for her people.

In the 1960s, a civil war broke out as some people banded together to try to rid the country of its military government. After thirty-six long years, the war finally ended in 1996. More than 200,000 people, mostly Maya, had been killed. The Peace Accords gave people hope that Guatemala might be able to achieve a new start. Though the country is still plagued by poverty and corruption, Guatemalans continue to show a determined spirit that has always carried them through.

Lake Atitlán

Land of Volcanoes and Earthquakes

A stretch of Guatemalan coastline

THE REPUBLIC OF GUATEMALA IS THE THIRD-LARGEST COUNtry in Central America after Nicaragua and Honduras. Still, it is not a large country—it is slightly smaller than the state of Tennessee. Mexico lies to the north and west of Guatemala. Belize is to the east, and Honduras and El Salvador are to the southeast. To the south, Guatemala has about 150 miles (240 km) of coastline along the Pacific Ocean. Eastern Guatemala has about 100 miles (160 km) of coastline along the Caribbean Sea. Its Caribbean coastline includes the low-lying Manabique Peninsula and part of the Bay of Amatique, a large inlet of the Gulf of Honduras.

Opposite: **Lake Atitlán is one of Guatemala's most popular attractions.**

Guatemala's Geographic Features

Area: 42,042 square miles (108,889 sq km)

Highest Elevation: Volcán Tajumulco, 13,846 feet (4,220 m)

Lowest Elevation: Sea level along the coasts

Longest River: Motagua, 250 miles (400 km)

Largest Lake: Izabal, 228 square miles (591 sq km)

Annual Average Temperature in the Highlands: 60°–70°F (16°–21°C)

Annual Average Temperature in the Lowlands: 70°–80°F (21°–27°C)

Annual Average Rainfall: varies from 30 to 200 inches (75 to 500 cm) according to region

Deadliest Earthquake in Recent Times: 1976

The Shaking Crossroads

Guatemala is in constant danger from earthquakes. Here's why: Earth's surface is broken up into several huge pieces called tectonic plates. These plates are constantly moving in relation to one another. The borders between tectonic plates are where most earthquakes occur. Guatemala rests at a point where three tectonic plates meet. No place in the country is totally safe from earthquakes. In southeast Guatemala, the North American Plate is constantly grinding against the Caribbean Plate. The line of this movement is known as the Motagua Fault. It extends across 80 percent of the country.

Jade Rush

The Motagua River (below) starts in the mountains north of Guatemala City and follows the Motagua Fault eastward for 250 miles (400 km) to Omoa Bay in the Gulf of Honduras. In 2002, the Motagua River valley became the site of a rush to find jade, a green stone favored by the Maya. The stone had been washed clear of the fault by the scouring action of the flood-waters following Hurricane Mitch in 1998.

Earthquakes strong enough to be felt shake the land near the Motagua Fault several times a year, but the area has no volcanic activity. The scene is different in the west of the country close to the Pacific Ocean. Here the Cocos Plate is forcing its way under the Caribbean Plate. This movement has pushed up a range of mountains along the coast.

The 1976 Earthquake

Before dawn on February 4, 1976, Guatemalans were wakened by a strong earthquake. The quake centered on the Motagua Fault, 93 miles (150 km) northeast of the capital. The first shock came at 3:03 A.M. It lasted 49 terrifying seconds and measured 7.5 on the Richter scale. The quake sent people scurrying into the streets. Another strong shock came at 3:30, just as people were returning to their homes to rescue their possessions.

The result was devastating. It is estimated that 23,000 people died, 76,000 were injured, and a million were left homeless. Piles of rubble covered thousands of homes, and much of the northern part of Guatemala City was ruined. In the countryside, some villages were spared, while others not far down the road were totally destroyed. It took the country years to recover from the disaster.

Houses dot the landscape of the Cordillera de los Cuchumatenes.

The Highlands

About two-thirds of Guatemala is mountainous, and most of the country's people live in the highlands. The capital, Guatemala City, lies on a plateau in the midst of the mountains at 4,850 feet (1,478 meters) above sea level.

A mountain range called the Cordillera de los Cuchumatenes reaches 12,589 feet (3,837 m) near the Mexican border. The range is the most extensive highland area in Central America. Lush rain forest covers the northern end of these mountains, where the annual rainfall exceeds 100 inches (250 centimeters).

The smoldering peak of Santiaguito

Much of the southern part of the country is dominated by a line of volcanoes. More than thirty volcanoes form a row extending from Tacaná on the Mexican border to Chingo near El Salvador. Three of these volcanoes are continuously active. Santa Maria is perhaps the most famous. It erupted violently in 1902, killing thousands of people. Fuego is also very active. Pacaya, which can be seen from Guatemala City, last erupted in 2002. Close to the Mexican border, another volcano, Tajumulco, is the highest point in Guatemala at 13,846 feet (4,220 m).

1902 Santa Maria Eruption

On October 25, 1902, Santa Maria exploded in a huge eruption that lasted between eighteen and twenty hours. Smoke and ash soared more than 17 miles (28 km) into the sky. The ash fell on an area covering 463,200 square miles (1.2 million sq km). As many as 7,500 people may have died as a result of the eruption. Many died from malaria. This disease is transmitted by mosquitoes, which flourished after the eruption. Normally, birds help control the mosquito population, but many were killed when Santa Maria erupted. The eruption left a giant crater in one side of Santa Maria. Since 1922, a smaller volcano known as Santiaguito has been growing from the base of the hole and is constantly active.

A mountain tableland stretches north and east of the volcanoes. Rivers have cut deep valleys through this region. Much of this expanse is isolated, as roads have not been built and large areas are covered with dense forest.

Lakes

Two mountain ranges, the Sierra de Santa Cruz and the Sierra de las Minas, reach toward Guatemala's narrow Caribbean coast. They form a basin filled by Lake Izabal, the largest lake in Guatemala and the third-largest natural lake in Central America. Lake Izabal is fed by the Polochic River and smaller rivers rising in the surrounding mountains. The western end of Lake Izabal is swampy. The eastern end leads to the Dulce River and a small lagoon before entering the Bay of Amatique.

Castillo San Felipe along Lake Izabal

Smaller lakes in the mountains to the west are famed for their beauty. Lake Atitlán is set in a depression formed by an ancient volcanic eruption. Three volcanoes overlook the lake today. Atitlán, which last erupted in 1853, is the highest, at 11,595 feet (3,534 m). Beside it rises Toliman, which has not erupted in recent times. Slightly to the west is the extinct San Pedro volcano. Another scenic mountain lake, Amatitlán, lies between Guatemala City and Pacaya volcano.

A breathtaking view of Lake Atitlán

An aerial view of Sierra del Lacandón, which is located in the Petén

The Lowlands

Guatemala has two distinct regions of lowlands. One, the Pacific Lowland, stretches out along the Pacific coast. Few people live in the Pacific Lowland, which is today mostly made up of large farms.

Guatemala's other lowland is much larger. This region, which covers all of northeastern Guatemala, is known as the Petén. Here, much of the land is made of limestone. Limestone is a kind of rock that dissolves easily. Slightly acidic water seeps into cracks in the rock and slowly dissolves it. This creates caves, craggy towers of rock, and deep holes called sinkholes. This curious scenery is called karst.

Usumacinta River

Parts of the Petén are very dry. They get little rainfall and have little soil. In these areas, only plants such as cactuses grow. But parts of the Petén are drenched with rain. In these areas, wet, broadleaf rain forest covers the land.

Along the western edge of the Petén, the Usumacinta River and its tributary, the Salinas, form the border with Mexico. At the point where it leaves Guatemala, the Usumacinta cuts through the Sierra de Lacandón, a range of low hills, in a series of canyons. The river drops 230 feet (70 m) in 90 miles (145 km) with rapids and low waterfalls.

The Legend of Quetzaltenango

Quetzaltenango lies in a mountainous region west of Guatemala City. Its name comes from two words, *quetzal*, which is a striking long-tailed bird that lives in Guatemala's forests, and *tenango*, which means "the place of." According to legend, the name Quetzaltenango dates to the time of the Spanish invasion of Guatemala.

In February 1524, the Spanish conquistador Pedro de Alvarado led an army into the highlands. There he met a native army led by the Maya hero Tecún Umán. According to the Maya, Tecún Umán wore a headdress of quetzal feathers and crowns of precious metals and jewels. They say he became an eagle with feathers on his body, wings, and crowns of gold, diamonds, and emeralds.

The young warrior arose in flight to attack Alvarado, stabbing him with his spear. Alvarado was astounded by the young warrior's beauty. He said he had never seen an Indian so handsome. So Alvarado named the spot Quetzaltenango, meaning the "place of the quetzal." Today, a statue of Tecún Umán stands guard at the entrance to the city.

Climate

Guatemala's climate varies partly according to the elevation. High on a plateau, Guatemala City has an average annual temperature of 67°F (19°C). Puerto Barrios on the Caribbean coast has an average temperature of 79°F (26.1°C). In much of the country, the rainy season lasts from May to November. But in the Petén, it rains year-round. Parts of the Petén get as much as 150 inches (380 cm) of rain per year. A big contrast to this is the semidesert in the Motagua Valley. One of the driest places in Central America, it receives less than 20 inches (50 cm) of rain per year, and temperatures have reached as high as 106°F (41°C).

Rain clouds over Tikal ruins in a Guatemalan jungle

A Look at Guatemala's Cities

Quetzaltenango (below) is Guatemala's fourth-largest city. Located in the highlands of southern Guatemala, it has fantastic mountain views, including of the Santa María volcano. Quetzaltenango is a center for the Quiché Maya people. It is also home to a lot of foreigners because it has many schools for learning Spanish. Quetzaltenango is notable for its cathedral, parts of which date to 1535.

Escuintla is a bustling city in the foothills of the mountains 36 miles (58 km) southwest of Guatemala City. With a population of 69,311, it is the fifth-largest city in Guatemala. The city's name is derived from

Itzcuintli, a dog kept by the Maya. The city is noted for its palm trees and warm climate. Escuintla is the wealthy hub of a region whose economy is based on cattle ranching, sugarcane, cottonseed, and a small oil refinery.

Flores (above) is the most important city in the Petén. It is built on an island in Lake Petén Itzá. A short causeway connects the island to the mainland. Flores is a small city, with a population of just 18,399. Every part of the island is covered with narrow cobblestone streets and colorful buildings. It is the capital of a region whose economy is based on forest products. Tourism is also important. Flores is a jumping-off point for many visitors to the nearby Maya ruins of Tikal.

Wild Guatemala

GUATEMALA HAS HIGH MOUNTAINS, LOWLANDS, AND
seacoasts. It has ecosystems ranging from deserts to sodden rain
forests. With all these different regions, it probably has the
greatest diversity of plant and animal life in Central America.

Plant Life

Thousands upon thousands of different species of plants grow
in Guatemala. These range from the mangrove trees that rise
from swamps along the coast to the cactus that grow in arid

Opposite: **A Ceiba tree**

**Cactus along the
Motagua River**

The National Tree

The ceiba was sacred to the Maya. It is one of the grandest trees in Central America. It can reach a height of 200 feet (60 m), and its enormous trunk can be as much as 6 feet (2 m) across.

A cloud forest near Fuentes Georginos

regions. The lush rain forests of the Petén host an incredible diversity of plant life. Huge ceiba trees, sapodilla, mahogany, and many types of palm grow in the rain forest. Other parts of the Petén are home to pine forests and grasslands.

Cloud forests thrive on some of Guatemala's mountain peaks. These tropical, higher elevation forests are almost always shrouded in mist. The constant wetness produces abundant life. Vines crisscross between trees. Mosses, ferns, and orchids coat the forest floor and tree trunks. Bromeliads burst wildly from the sides of trees. Like many plants in the cloud forest, bromeliads grow directly on trees rather than in the soil. They get all their moisture and nutrients from rain

and the air. The broad leaves of the bromeliads capture a great deal of the rain. At the center of the plant are often pools of water that make good homes for frogs.

Animal Life

More than 250 different kinds of mammals live in Guatemala. Some are large, such as the jaguar, puma, and mountain lion. Baird's tapir can weigh up to 900 pounds (400 kilos). It looks a little like a large pig with a long snout, but it is more closely

Baird's tapir live in Guatemala.

A howler monkey

related to a horse. Howler monkeys are also common. They get their name from the shouts they let out when other monkeys enter their territory. The smaller spider monkeys seem to be everywhere in Guatemala. Other common creatures are ant-eaters, peccaries, and coatimundi, which are similar to raccoons.

Guatemala is home to 750 kinds of birds, including harpy eagles, hummingbirds, parrots, and macaws. At 5 feet (1.5 m) tall, the Jabirú stork is one of the largest bird in the Western Hemisphere. It flies into Guatemala from Mexico in November to build its nests in treetops.

Guatemala's national bird, the resplendent quetzal, is one of the most beautiful birds of Central America. These birds are small, about 14 inches (35 cm) long, but their tails can add another 36 inches (91 cm). Both males and females are a shiny green. The males also have a red crest and breast. The resplendent quetzal lives in high mountain cloud forests. The bird is threatened because much of its forest habitat has been destroyed. It is now restricted to just a few areas.

Saving the National Bird

Mario Dary Rivera, the one-time director of Guatemala's San Carlos University, was concerned that the destruction of forests was leaving animals with nowhere to live. He set about searching for a site that could become a sanctuary for the resplendent quetzal, Guatemala's national bird. In 1976–77, he found an area of dense cloud forest between the Sierra de Chuacús and the Sierra de las Minas. The rugged land has abundant crystal clear water. It is an area of dripping forests filled with many ferns, mosses, and orchids. The site was named for Dary, but it is known locally as the Quetzal Reserve. It offers visitors a chance to walk through untouched mountain forests where tropical birds have sought refuge.

The Atitlán Giant Grebe

For years, ornithologists—scientists who study birds—were drawn to Lake Atitlán, where they hoped to spot the Atitlán giant grebe. The grebe family is a group of diving birds that propel themselves using their feet. They feed on small fish, insect larvae, and other water creatures. The grebes range in size from 8 to 31 inches (20 to 78 cm). The Atitlán giant grebe, which was found only on Lake Atitlán, was one of the larger species of grebe. It was often known as a flightless grebe, because it was a very weak flyer.

In 1960, about 200 Atitlán giant grebes remained. In that year, the largemouth bass was introduced to the lake. It was hoped that the bass would increase tourism because people would come to fish. But largemouth bass will eat practically anything. They ate so much, in fact, that there was little left for the grebes. The number of Atitlán giant grebes dropped quickly. By 1986, they were gone entirely. This unique bird is now extinct.

Protected Areas

Guatemala has nearly 100 protected areas, from remote wildlife refuges to popular national parks. These areas are vital in protecting Guatemala's incredible array of plant and animal life.

The Sierra de las Minas is a mountain chain 81 miles (130 km) long. The entire area is a national park. Plant life in the region is especially rich, with more than 2,000 species. The Sierra de las Minas region is also home to 885 species of mammals, birds, and reptiles. The region can support these many species because of its incredible diversity of climate and environment. Parts of the Sierra de las Minas are among the driest places in Central America. These areas are filled with thorny plants such as acacia and cactus. But at higher elevations, the reserve is home to what is probably the largest unbroken cloud forest in Central America. Cloud forests are wet tropical mountain forests that are noted for being shrouded in clouds even during the dry season. The mountain peaks receive as much as 160 inches (400 cm) of rain per year.

A protected rain forest in the
Petén region

Muscovy duck

The Petén region covers more than a third of Guatemala. It is one of the last remaining large wildland areas in Central America. At one time, much of Petén was covered by forest. Today, less than half those forests remain. The Maya Biosphere Reserve occupies the northern section of Petén and amounts to about 15 percent of the country. It is home to toucans, parrots, and other brightly colored birds, including the Petén turkey, which looks something like a peacock. The reserve is also home to spider monkeys, howler monkeys, and gray foxes. A few puma still live in the Petén, but they usually stay far away from where people are.

Guatemala's Caribbean coast faces the Gulf of Honduras. A long, thin peninsula juts out from the coast, separating the gulf from Amatique Bay. It is home to the Punta de Manabique Wildlife Refuge. This refuge is the last nesting place in the Caribbean for the muscovy duck, a large black duck with red nodules on parts of its head. Many of the animals that once lived in this region—including the American crocodile, two species of peccary (a wild pig), the jaguar, and the manatee, or sea cow—are becoming increasingly rare. The environment is threatened by livestock ranching and development for tourism.

The Monterrico Nature Reserve lies on the Pacific coast. The reserve is a haven for alligator-like caimans, iguanas, and armadillos. Many types of birds pass through the reserve, including pink flamingos. The reserve is perhaps most famous as a nesting place for endangered turtles. The leatherback, olive ridley, and Baule sea turtles all lay their eggs on the beach in the reserve.

Sea turtle hatchlings

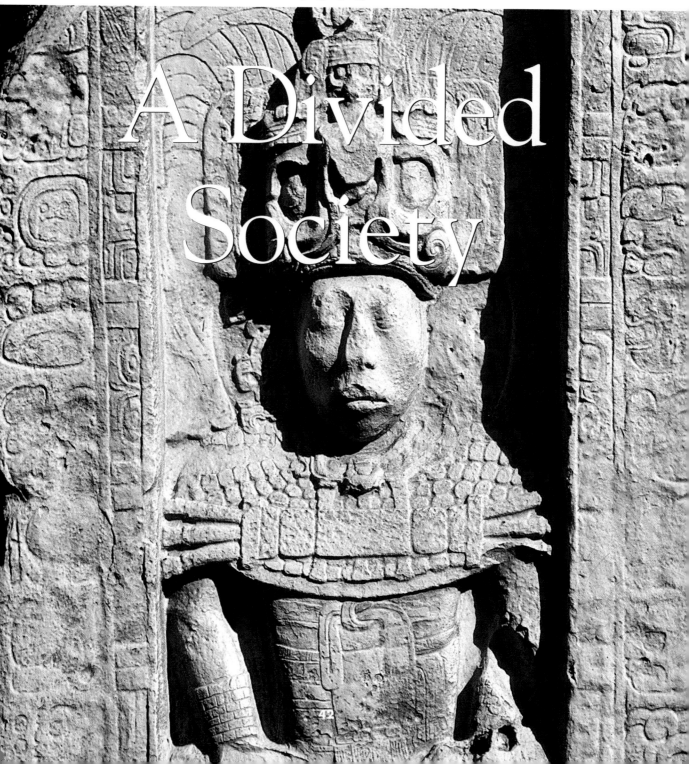

A Divided Society

THE FIRST PEOPLE IN THE AMERICAS ARRIVED FROM ASIA between 10,000 and 30,000 years ago. At the time, the planet was in the midst of an ice age. So much water froze into ice that sea levels dropped, and a land bridge rose above the sea between what is now Russia and Alaska. People walked across this bridge and spread out across North and South America. They survived by hunting and fishing. Stone tools and spear points dating from around 9000 B.C. have been found in the Guatemalan highlands. From about 1000 B.C., people in Guatemala were living in villages. They grew crops of corn, beans, and squash. Among these early Guatemalans were the Maya. One of the largest populations was at Kaminaljuyu, on the outskirts of present-day Guatemala City.

Opposite: **A reproduction carving from Piedras Negras**

Mayan art showing the profile of a male figure

The World of the Maya

The Maya developed the most advanced civilization in Central America at the time. Their classical period lasted from about A.D. 250 to about 900. Their main cities and ceremonial centers were filled with pyramids, temples, palaces, plazas, and markets. At its height, the city of Tikal was home to between 50,000 and 100,000 Maya people. The Maya had an aggressive culture controlled by priests and nobles. Cities, including Tikal, Uaxactun, El Mirador, and Quirigua, were frequently at war with each other. Victims of war were sometimes tortured and sacrificed to the gods.

There was, however, another side to the Maya. They were brilliant artists and scientists. Their magnificent cities were built with only the most basic tools of flint and hard stones. They produced fine pottery, sculptures, carvings, weavings, and paintings. They developed a system of writing. Hieroglyphs on stone monuments in many sites record their history. The Maya were also accomplished farmers. They used irrigation and fertilizers to grow enough crops to feed the people in their large cities.

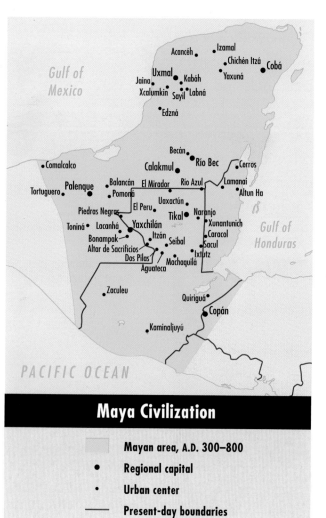

Maya Civilization

- Mayan area, A.D. 300–800
- • Regional capital
- · Urban center
- — Present-day boundaries

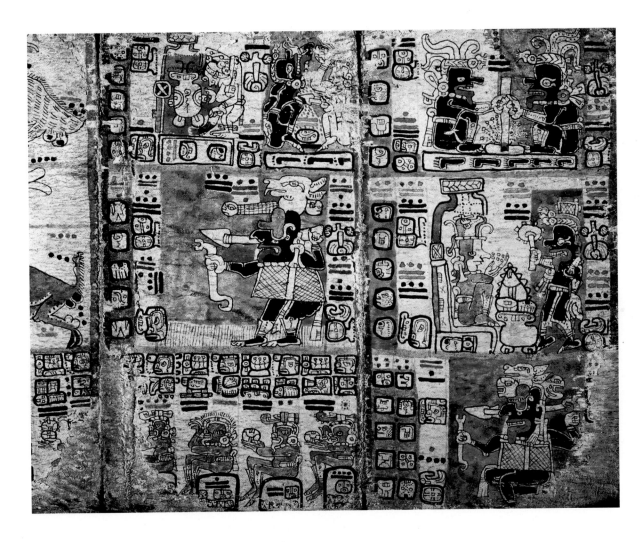

The Maya's major scientific achievement was the under-standing of time, mathematics, and astronomy. They used the zero before Europeans did. They also devised an accurate cal-endar with two cycles. One was a solar cycle of 365 days. The other was a sacred cycle of 260 days. This calendar was used to foretell the future and avoid bad luck. Only priests trained in astrology could read the sacred calendar.

The Maya Ballgame

Most Maya sites have a ball court. Two teams of players tried to get a large rubber ball through a stone ring on the side of the court. It is thought that the players were supposed to keep the ball in the air without using their hands or feet. The best shots were made from the hip. Because of the speed and weight of the ball, the game was very dangerous. Players protected themselves with hip pads, kneepads, and gloves. The Maya ballgame was a serious matter. Members of the losing team were sometimes killed.

After 900, the Maya civilization declined. Many experts believe this may have been because of severe droughts that struck the region. Overpopulation and warfare among the various Maya groups may have also caused the decline. For whatever reason, the Maya abandoned their great cities. The jungle soon covered their pyramids and monuments.

Spanish Conquest

By the time the Spaniards arrived in Guatemala in the early sixteenth century, the Maya were made up of many warring tribes. The strongest and largest was the Quiché, who had recently defeated their main rivals, the Cakchiquel. None of the Mayan tribes, however, were any match for Pedro de Alvarado, the Spanish soldier sent to Guatemala by Hernan Cortés, the conqueror of Mexico. Ambitious, cunning, and cruel, Alvarado arrived in Guatemala in 1523 with 120 horsemen, 173 horses, 300 soldiers, and some Mexican warriors. Although confronted by some 30,000 Quiché warriors, the Spanish horses and guns proved too much, and the Quiché were soundly defeated. The Spaniards had little trouble dealing with the remaining tribes.

Guatemala was a Spanish colony for about 300 years. Unlike Mexico and Peru, it did not have vast gold and other riches. Instead, land was the most prized possession. After seizing the Maya's land, the Spanish soon set up the *encomienda* system in Guatemala. Under this system, a few leading Spaniards were given vast estates, and the Maya were forced to work the land. Indians who refused to work were killed. The encomienda system virtually enslaved the Maya.

In time, the encomienda owners became so powerful and brutal that King Carlos V of Spain decided to put a stop to it. In 1542, he enacted the New Laws. These laws officially ended forced labor. The laws also stated that the encomienda estates could not be passed down from father to son.

The ancient city of Guatemala

Though this was supposed to improve the plight of the Maya, in reality the laws were not very effective. By this time, Guatemala already had a rigid power structure. At the top of the ladder were Spaniards born in Europe. They held the most authority. Below them were people of purely Spanish heritage who had been born in Guatemala. Next came the ladinos, people of mixed Spanish and Mayan heritage. And at the very bottom of Guatemalan society were the Maya themselves.

The arrival of the Spaniards in Guatemala also brought Catholicism to the region. Priests worked to try to convert the Indians to Christianity. Though many Maya became Catholic, most intertwined their Catholic beliefs with their traditional religion. The Catholic Church was also given a great deal of land in Guatemala. It became wealthy and powerful.

In the late 1600s, the Spaniards created hundreds of new towns and villages. The native people were forced to live in these villages, where they became a source of labor that could

Antigua, the Colonial Capital

The first two Spanish capital towns in Guatemala were destroyed in earthquakes. The third was founded in 1543. Like the first two, it was named Santiago de los Caballeros de Guatemala. It became Spain's main administrative, religious, and political center in the Americas and the most important city in colonial Central America. Santiago, which was home to 60,000 people, was filled with churches, schools, and hospitals. It had a university, a printing press, and a newspaper. Bishops, noblemen, wealthy merchants,

and politicians built grand palaces and mansions in the capital. It was also home to famous sculptors, painters, writers, and craftsmen.

The city suffered moderate shaking for years before an earthquake demolished most of it in 1773. Three years later, the capital was moved to Guatemala City, and Santiago became Antigua Guatemala. Fortunately, enough buildings and ruins remain today for visitors to appreciate the grandeur of the old city.

easily be exploited. Some Maya managed to escape to remote areas, where they lived in their own independent communities.

Independence

By the beginning of the nineteenth century, most colonies in Latin America wanted independence from Spain. In some colonies, the fight for independence involved violent, lengthy wars. Guatemala opted for a peaceful declaration of independence in 1821. Shortly after, however, it was annexed by Mexico, itself a newly independent republic. The association lasted barely a year.

In 1823, Guatemala joined the newly created United Provinces of Central America. Costa Rica, Honduras, Nicaragua, and El Salvador were also part of this union, which had its capital in Guatemala City. From the beginning, this union was split between two groups. The conservatives had the support of the Catholic Church and the large landowners. The liberals wanted to lessen the power of the Church and improve the lot of the ladinos and the Maya. These tensions proved too much for the United Provinces. The union lasted only until 1840, before splitting into separate countries.

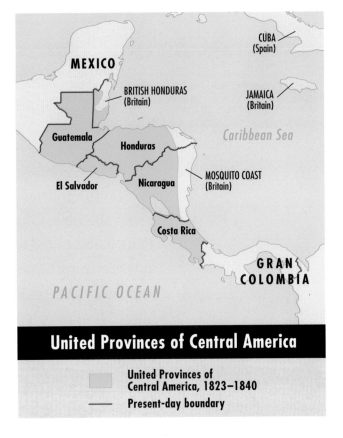

United Provinces of Central America

United Provinces of
Central America, 1823–1840
——— Present-day boundary

Justo Rufino Barrios

A conservative, charismatic leader named José Rafael Carrera soon emerged in Guatemala. With the support of the Catholic Church and landowners, he defeated the liberals. In 1844, he became Guatemala's first president, ensuring that power remained with his supporters. He continued on as president until his death in 1865.

Coffee Boom

In 1871, a military commander named Justo Rufino Barrios led a liberal revolt. He soon became president and tried to reform the nation. Barrios took education out of the hands of the Catholic Church and made it the responsibility of the government. He also reduced the power of the Church and confiscated its lands. But Barrios ruled as a dictator, and his policies led to greater inequality in Guatemala.

At the time, Guatemala's coffee industry was booming. By 1870, it accounted for about half the country's exports. Barrios did everything he could to support the coffee industry. Indians were kicked off their land to make way for coffee plantations. Many Maya were forced to work on the plantations. In reality, a small group of plantation owners controlled the country. Many villages rose up in revolt, but the army put down these rebellions. Barrios was killed in 1885. By this time, Guatemala had its first railway network to ferry coffee beans to the ports and a coffee industry that accounted for more than 80 percent of its exports.

Banana Republic

Manuel Estrada Cabrera became president of Guatemala in 1898. He was a dictator who used the army, the secret police, and rigged elections to stay in power. Under his heavy-handed rule, Guatemala made some progress. Schools were built. Agricultural production increased. But at

Manuel Estrada Cabrera

the same time, Cabrera stole from the government and did nothing to improve the plight of the Maya. His presidency was marked by widespread U.S. investment in the Guatemalan economy, in particular by the United Fruit Company. This

The United Fruit Company

In 1871, a young American named Minor Keith went to Costa Rica to build a railroad. Alongside the tracks he planted bananas, a fruit then hardly known in the United States. He soon owned three banana companies, and in 1899, he and some partners formed the United Fruit Company (UFC), the largest banana company in the world. The UFC set up banana plantations throughout Central and South America and the Caribbean.

The UFC first moved into Guatemala in 1901, with the exclusive right to transport mail between Guatemala and the United States. Soon, the company was also growing bananas there. The UFC was then hired to build the railroad and telegraph lines between Guatemala City and Puerto Barrios. Part of the deal was the government gave the company land on either side of the railroad track. The company also received a 99-year tax break.

In 1924, the company was granted more land by the Guatemalan government, which it used for large-scale banana plantations. By the 1930s, the United Fruit Company's control over the country's railway network also gave it control over the coffee industry. The UFC made vast profits from its plantations and other investments. It had so much influence in some Central American countries that they were called banana republics.

company gained so much control in so many parts of the Guatemalan economy that it became known as *El Pulpo*, "the Octopus."

Cabrera was overthrown in 1920. He was followed by a string of presidents who had little impact on the nation. Then in 1931, Jorge Ubico Castañeda came to power. He improved health care and education and built an extensive network of roads. But he too was a tyrant and a firm supporter of the landowners and the United Fruit Company. He did little for the poor. In fact, he passed a law requiring that all peasants who didn't own land be forced to work 150 days a year. This gave the landowners even more power over the Maya. If there was no work to be done on the land, the peasants were forced to build roads or work on other government projects. Ubico was overthrown in 1944. By this time, there was a strong desire among the people for a true democratic government. In that same year, Guatemala held its first genuine elections.

Jorge Ubico

Ten Years of Spring

University professor Juan José Arévalo won the elections. This began a period that Guatemalans refer to as "Ten Years of Spring." Arévalo enacted many reforms. The country got a new constitution, and most people were able to vote for the first time. A large chunk of the national budget went toward schools and hospitals. Workers were given the right to form unions and to strike. The law forcing peasants to work was abolished. Neither the landowners nor the United Fruit Company welcomed these measures. Arévalo survived his full term in office, despite numerous plots to overthrow him.

Captain Jacobo Arbenz

He was succeeded by Jacobo Arbenz Guzman. Arbenz wanted to transform Guatemala into a modern country. At the time, just 2.2 percent of the population owned over 70 percent of the land. Arbenz passed a land reform law in 1952. Under this law, land that was not being used to grow crops was taken away from rich landowners and the United Fruit Company and given to about 100,000 peasant families. The landowners were paid for the land, but they were still furious.

The United Fruit Company, the Catholic Church, large landowners, and most of the army all despised Arbenz. So did the United States government, which thought he was leaning toward communism, and supported a plot to overthrow him. Pressure built on Arbenz, and he resigned in June 1954.

Military Government

The military dominated Guatemalan politics for the next thirty years. It supported the wealthy landowners and quickly stopped any move to help the poor. In 1954, President Castillo Armas reversed the reforms of the previous ten years.

Nearly all the land handed out to the peasants was returned to the landowners. People who could not read, mostly the Maya, were deprived of the vote, and some political parties were banned. Large numbers of people who backed reforms were arrested, jailed, or killed.

Guatemala's first guerrilla movement had been formed in 1960. This unofficial army wanted to overthrow the government and return to democracy. The group attracted large numbers of students and peasants. It later joined forces with another group and became known as the Armed Rebel Forces. This was the beginning of the longest civil war in Latin American history. On the one side were the guerrillas, who operated from bases in the eastern highlands and Guatemala City. On the other side were the army, right-wing parties, landowners, and the United States. In the late 1960s, the army wiped out many peasant communities and almost eliminated the guerrillas. But the guerrillas regrouped, again building up support among the peasants.

The army received equipment and training from the United States. In Guatemala, the army was supported by Civil Defense Patrols. The job of the patrols was to spy on neighbors and report back to the army. No one felt safe from informers.

The civil war reached its peak in the early 1980s. During a reign of terror by both General Romero Lucas Garcia, from 1978 to 1982, and General Efrain Rios Montt, from 1982 to 1983, about 30,000 people were killed. Maya peasants were massacred by the hundreds, and villages were burnt to the ground. Among other groups targeted and killed were students, teachers, academics, lawyers, union leaders, and journalists. Tens of thousands of refugees fled into Mexico. Another 200,000 people were forced from their homes. They had nowhere to go and became refugees inside Guatemala. The Civil Defense Patrols pushed them into new "model villages" in tightly controlled military zones.

Rigoberta Menchú Tum

Rigoberta Menchú Tum was awarded the Nobel Peace Prize in 1992, the youngest person ever to receive it.

She was given the award to honor her work fighting for social justice and rights of native people.

Menchú was born in 1959 into a family of Quiché Maya peasants. When she was young, she worked on the family's small fields in the highlands and on coffee plantations on the Pacific Coast.

As a young woman, she was very active in women's rights and social reform movements. Other members of her family were also involved. Her father, brother, and mother were later arrested, tortured, and killed by the army. As Menchú became more prominent in the fight for social justice, her life too was under threat. In 1981, she fled to Mexico. From there, she continued to promote the rights of native people and to organize resistance against the military.

In 1983, her autobiography *I, Rigoberta Menchú, an Indian woman in Guatemala,* was published. It is a gripping account of poor peasant life and the atrocities committed by the Guatemalan army in the 1970s. In the years since its publication, some critics have questioned the truth of some of her claims. Today, she is a goodwill ambassador for the United Nations. She has also worked with the Guatemalan government promoting the Peace Accords.

Return to Democracy

In 1983, Rios Montt, one of Guatemala's most brutal leaders, was overthrown. Two years later, Vinicio Cerezo Arévalo was elected the first civilian president in twenty years. His presidency allowed for a relative period of peace, although the army was still largely in control. By the end of the presidency, however, violence was again on the increase.

The Peace Process

Against a background of continuing violence, talks began in 1987 between the government and the guerillas. The guerrillas demanded that the Civil Defense Patrols be disbanded. They also wanted an investigation into human rights abuses. The government, meanwhile, insisted the guerrillas disarm before negotiations would begin.

The Fight for Human Rights

In the mid-1980s, several organizations formed to protest the conditions in which most Maya lived. They also supported the many Maya who had lost family members in the civil war. In 1986, about 3,000 people took part in a protest to demand information about the fate of thousands of people who had "disappeared"— they had been arrested or killed without any word to the families. The government promised to investigate. The Catholic Church lent its support to the campaigns. Maya widows frequently took to the streets in Guatemala City in their colorful traditional dress, carrying their babies, to protest the ongoing violence and repression.

Of particular concern were the Maya families who had fled army massacres in the 1980s to live in the rain forests. Living in isolation, they had their own schools and health clinics. The army was a constant threat. When patrols got too close, these communities packed their belongings and moved on. The army then destroyed everything, burning houses, pulling up crops, killing animals, and poisoning water wells. In the early 1990s, some communities made their plight known to the outside world. They got help from human rights organizations and the Catholic Church. Since 1996, many have settled back into normal rural life.

Violence and massacres again increased in the early 1990s, largely under orders from the military and businesspeople who were against tax increases and talks with the guerrillas. Talks between the government and the guerillas finally began to progress in 1994, when the United Nations was invited to take part.

In 1996, a peace agreement was reached and was signed by the new president, Álvaro Arzú. The guerillas agreed to give up their arms, while the government committed itself to democracy. The Peace Accords included an agreement to resettle people displaced by the war and to investigate human rights abuses by the military. The Peace Accords also acknowledged that the Maya had been exploited and discriminated against. There were other agreements in the document as well. Land reform would be made. A new bank would be set up that would supply funds for peasants to buy land. The health and education budget was to double over the next four years, largely by increasing taxes. The government also agreed to disarm the Civil Defense Patrols and create a new civilian police force. The Peace Accords finally brought to an end Guatemala's thirty-six-year civil war, in which an estimated 200,000 people died.

A UN Canadian military observer (right) is greeted by a guerrilla fighter in 1997.

Governing
Guatemala

W HEN ÁLVARO ARZÚ BECAME PRESIDENT IN 1996, HE set about modernizing the government and introducing social reform. In the aftermath of the civil war, there was much to do. Investigations revealed that 90 percent of the human rights abuses during the war had been committed by the army and other government forces. Of the 200,000 who died during the conflict, over 80 percent were unarmed Maya men, women, and children. But few members of the armed forces were put on trial for their crimes. And in one case, twenty-five officers convicted of massacring thirteen civilians were given jail sentences of just five years. The public was outraged.

Opposite: **Guard at the National Palace**

The National Flag

Guatemala's national flag has three vertical bands. The bands on the sides are blue; the one in the middle is white. The blue bands stand for the Caribbean Sea and Pacific Ocean. The national coat of arms is in the middle of the white band, with a quetzal symbolizing freedom. A pair of crossed rifles and crossed swords represent the defense of liberty, and a scroll bears the inscription *Libertad 15 de Septiembre de 1821*, the date of Guatemalan independence.

Since then, Guatemalan leaders have made promises to reform the armed forces and protect human rights. Unfortunately, abuses and corruption have continued. In 2003, Oscar Berger was elected president after pledging to reduce corruption. But the nation has a long way to go before it achieves a truly peaceful and democratic government.

The Constitution

Guatemala's constitution was drawn up in 1984, put into effect in 1986, and amended in 1993. Under the constitution, the government has three branches. The executive is made up of the president and the Council of Ministers. The legislative branch consists of a one-house congress. The judicial branch is responsible for legal administration. Voting is required for all adults at least eighteen years old who are not serving on active duty with the armed forces or police. Voting is optional for people who cannot read and write.

The President and Congress

The president of Guatemala is elected to a four-year term and cannot be reelected to a second term. The vice president is also elected to a four-year term. He or she can run for president after being out of office for four years. The Council of Ministers are appointed by the president. Each minister heads a department such as foreign affairs or public health and welfare. Congress is made up of 158 deputies who are elected to four-year terms. They may be reelected for one additional term, but not immediately after the first term.

Justices in Guatemala's Supreme Court

The Judicial System

Legal cases begin with Judges of Peace or in Courts of First Instance. Appeals are heard by the Court of Second Instance. Guatemala's highest court is the Supreme Court. The Supreme Court and these lower courts handle civil and criminal cases. Another court deals with constitutional matters.

NATIONAL GOVERNMENT OF GUATEMALA

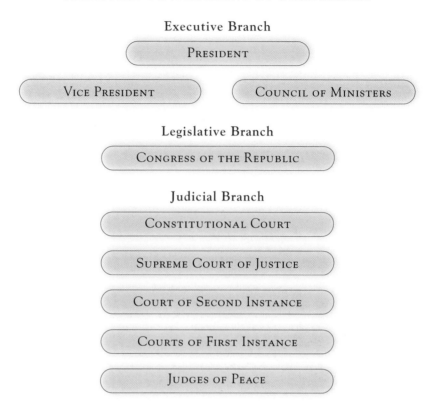

Executive Branch

PRESIDENT

VICE PRESIDENT

COUNCIL OF MINISTERS

Legislative Branch

CONGRESS OF THE REPUBLIC

Judicial Branch

CONSTITUTIONAL COURT

SUPREME COURT OF JUSTICE

COURT OF SECOND INSTANCE

COURTS OF FIRST INSTANCE

JUDGES OF PEACE

The Supreme Court has thirteen judges who are in office for five years. They are elected by the Congress from a list submitted by law school officials, an association of lawyers, and appellate judges. The Supreme Court nominates all other judges.

Regional and Local Government

Guatemala has twenty-two administrative subdivisions. Each is headed by a governor appointed by the president.

Guatemala City and 331 other cities and towns are governed by elected mayors or councils for four-year terms.

The Belize Border Question

Guatemala had a long-running dispute with Belize, its neighbor to the east. For much of its history, Belize was a British colony. In 1859, a treaty established the border between Belize and Guatemala. Part of this agreement was that Great Britain would build a road from Guatemala City to Belize, but the road was never built. As a result of this dispute, Guatemala claimed part of Belize.

The dispute grew more serious in 1964, when Belize became a self-governing colony. Guatemala's government broke off diplomatic relations with Great Britain and hinted at war. Belize became independent in 1981, but it was not until ten years later that Guatemala recognized Belizean independence. To this day, tensions between the two countries remain high, and the dispute still has not been resolved.

The National Anthem

The words to Guatemala's national anthem, "Guatemala Feliz" ("Guatemala, Be Praised"), were written by José Joaquín Palma. The music is by Rafael Alvarez Ovalle. The song was adopted as the national anthem in 1896.

Spanish Lyrics

¡Guatemala feliz! que tus aras
No profane jamás el verdugo;
Ni haya esclavos que laman el yugo
Ni tiranos que escupan tu faz.
Si mañana tu suelo sagrado
Lo amenaza invasión extranjera,
Libre al viento tu hermosa bandera
A vencer o a morir llamará.
Libre al viento tu hermosa bandera
A vencer o a morir llamará;
Que tu pueblo con ánima fiera
Antes meurto q'esclavo será.

English Lyrics

Fortunate Guatemala! May your altars
Never be profaned by cruel men.
May there never be slaves who submit to their yoke,
Or tyrants who deride you.
If tomorrow your sacred soil
Should be threatened by foreign invasion,
Your fair flag, flying freely in the wind,
Will call to you: Conquer or die.
Your fair flag, flying freely in the wind,
Will call to you: Conquer or die.
For your people, with heart and soul,
Would prefer death to slavery.

Guatemala City: Did You Know?

Guatemala City was founded in 1776, three years after the previous capital had been destroyed in an earthquake. It too has been severely damaged by earthquakes, and much of the city was rebuilt in 1917 and 1918. With a population of almost one million, Guatemala City is the nation's largest city. Guatemala's next two largest cities, Mixco and Villa Nueva, are both suburbs of Guatemala City.

Guatemala City is divided into twenty-one zones. Zone 1, the oldest part of the city, is in the north. The modern city—including the wealthy residential zones 9, 10, and 14—is in the south.

At the heart of Zone 1 is the Parque Central (below), the central plaza, which is dominated by the National Palace and the cathedral. The National Palace houses the offices of the president and his ministers.

Murals showing scenes from Guatemalan history decorate the walls of the grand rooms. The country's major museums are also in Guatemala City. The Museum of Archaeology and Ethnology has a superb collection of ancient Mayan artifacts. Highlights include an ancient throne and a reconstruction of a tomb.

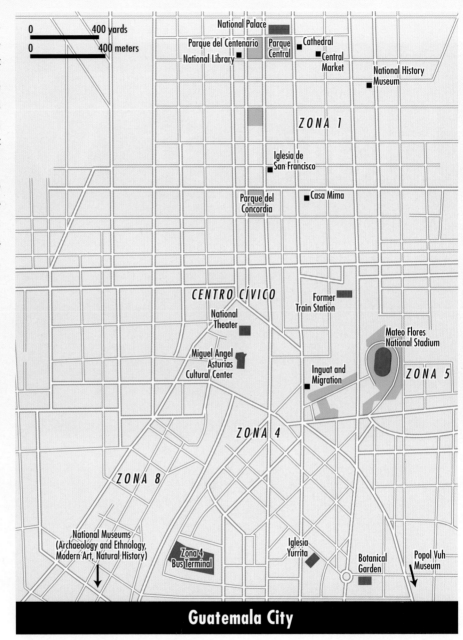

0   400 yards
0   400 meters

National Palace
Parque del Centenario
National Library
Parque Central
Cathedral
Central Market
National History Museum

ZONA 1

Iglesia de San Francisco

Parque del Concordia
Casa Mima

CENTRO CÍVICO

Former Train Station

National Theater

Mateo Flores National Stadium

Miguel Angel Asturias Cultural Center

Inguat and Migration

ZONA 5

ZONA 4

ZONA 8

National Museums (Archaeology and Ethnology, Modern Art, Natural History)

Zona 4 Bus Terminal

Iglesia Yurrita

Botanical Garden

Popol Vuh Museum

Guatemala City

Hard at Work

After the Peace Accords were signed in 1996, Guatemala was in a good position to develop its economy. The United States and other nations pledged millions of dollars toward helping the country rebuild. For a short time, the economy improved rapidly. Then in 1998, coffee prices collapsed. That same year, Hurricane Mitch caused much destruction in Guatemala. In addition, foreign companies were slow to invest in Guatemala's economy because of the ongoing violence and corruption. Nonetheless, the economy has continued, slowly, to improve.

Opposite: **A bean crop at a highland farm**

The aftermath of Hurricane Mitch

The Land Issue

Guatemala's economy faces thorny problems. Today, some 75 percent of Guatemalans live in poverty. The unequal distribution of land is one of the main causes. Roughly 70 percent of all productive farmland is owned by just 2.2 percent of the population. And less than 15 percent of Guatemala's land is suitable for farming. The most fertile land is in the Motagua Valley and along the southern coast. These regions are home to huge cotton, banana, and sugar plantations, along with cattle ranches and groves of rubber trees.

Farmers in Guatemala

Money Facts

Guatemala's basic unit of money is the Guatemala quetzal. The quetzal is divided into 100 centavos. Notes are in denominations of 100, 50, 20, 10, 1, and $\frac{1}{2}$ quetzals. Coins are in denominations of 25, 10, 5, and 1 centavos. The U.S. dollar also became an official currency in Guatemala in 2001.

All Guatemalan paper money has a picture of the colorful quetzal. The 5 quetzal note has a portrait of Justo Rufino Barrios, president from 1873 to 1885. The note is dedicated to the theme of education because he was the man who made elementary school free and mandatory. Barrios also said education should be run by the state, not the church. The reverse side of the note shows schoolchildren, with one boy in traditional Maya dress.

But two-thirds of Guatemalans live in the highlands. There the land is divided into small plots. Nearly 90 percent of these plots are too small to provide food for the families, much less have any left over to sell in local markets. Yet even these tiny plots of land are constantly under threat as more land is taken up to grow moneymaking crops for export.

Imports and Exports

The United States is Guatemala's main trading partner, providing 36 percent of its imports and receiving 30 percent of its

What Guatemala Grows, Makes, and Mines

Agriculture

Sugarcane	17,500,000 metric tons
Corn	1,050,000 metric tons
Bananas	940,000 metric tons

Manufacturing

Cement production	2,039,000 metric tons
Raw sugar	1,682,000 metric tons
Cigarettes	4,262,000 million

Mining

Petroleum	8,900,000 barrels

exports. Guatemala also imports goods from Mexico, South Korea, El Salvador, and China. Guatemala's main imports are fuel, electricity, machinery and transportation equipment, construction material, and fertilizers. Guatemala also exports a lot of goods to other Central American countries.

In 2000, Guatemala signed a free-trade agreement with Mexico, El Salvador, and Honduras. This created a much larger market where Guatemala can sell its goods without restrictions.

Agriculture

Agriculture, including forestry and fishing, is big business in Guatemala. It accounts for about a quarter of the value of all goods and services produced in Guatemala each year. About half the workforce works in agriculture, and agricultural products make up about two-thirds of Guatemala's exports. Sugar, coffee, and bananas are the main exports. These are Guatemala's traditional crops. But now the country also exports other fruits, winter vegetables, cut flowers, and plants. Guatemala is one of the world's major producers of a spice called cardamom. Cattle, pigs, and sheep are the main livestock raised in Guatemala.

A worker unloads boxes of fruit from a plantation truck.

Guatemala's forests are a huge resource. The main forest products are rubber, wood used to make furniture, and *chicle*, a gum from the sapodilla tree that is used to make chewing gum. Guatemala's fishing industry is fairly small, but shrimp is a common export.

Coffee Crisis

In 2001, the price of coffee fell from over $1 a pound to less than $0.50 a pound. The price drop was a disaster for many Central American countries. Guatemala lost about 250,000 of its 650,000 coffee-industry jobs. Many coffee farms in the

A Guatemalan farmer sowing coffee seedlings

highlands were abandoned or turned over to another crop. Former coffee workers, some from families who had been involved in coffee for a hundred years, left for the cities. Others moved to Mexico or the United States to find work.

Guatemalan coffee has always been highly rated. It is traditionally grown in the shade of large trees. This way, the coffee takes longer to grow, but it develops a richer flavor. After the coffee crisis, some of the farmers decided to focus on growing only top-quality coffee. This takes more time and effort, but coffee exports are once again increasing—they rose from $233 million in 2002 to $300 million in 2004.

Expanding Industry

Industry—which includes mining, manufacturing, construction, and power—employs about 15 percent of

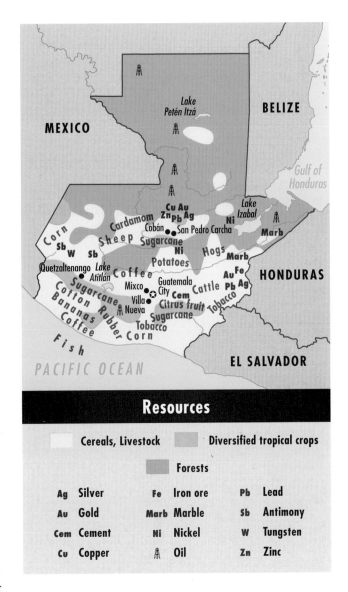

MEXICO
BELIZE
Lake Petén Itzá
Gulf of Honduras
Cu Au
Zn Pb Ag
Lake Izabal
Cardamom
Cobán
San Pedro Carcha
Marb
Corn
Sheep
Sugarcane
Ni
Hogs
Marb
Sb
W
Sb
Potatoes
Quetzaltenango
Lake Atitlán
Coffee
Au Fe
HONDURAS
Guatemala
Sugarcane
Mixco
City
Cattle
Pb Ag
Cotton
Rubber
Villa
Cem
Tobacco
Bananas
Nueva
Citrus fruit
Coffee
Sugarcane
Tobacco
Corn
Fish
PACIFIC OCEAN
EL SALVADOR

Resources

| Cereals, Livestock | | Diversified tropical crops |

| Forests |

Ag	Silver	Fe	Iron ore	Pb	Lead
Au	Gold	Marb	Marble	Sb	Antimony
Cem	Cement	Ni	Nickel	W	Tungsten
Cu	Copper	⚒	Oil	Zn	Zinc

the workers in Guatemala. Mining is only a small part of Guatemala's economy. The main product is oil, which is brought up from the ground in the Petén. Lead, zinc, and antimony are also mined on a small scale.

Manufacturing has been on the increase since the 1980s. The main products are processed foods, textiles, plastic and paper products, pharmaceuticals, and chemicals. Most of the factories are based in and around Guatemala City. In the late 1990s, there was rapid growth in *maquiladores*, factories owned by Guatemalan and foreign companies that make products for export. The plants, which are exempt from many taxes, employ hundreds of workers cheaply. Most Guatemalan maquiladores produce clothing.

Tourism

In 2004, services industries made up 58 percent of Guatemala's economy. Service industries include such things as banks, government agencies, communication companies, and tourism. Tourism is still a small industry in Guatemala. Many would-be visitors were scared off by the country's long civil war and years of upheaval. In 2001, fewer than a million tourists visited Guatemala, but they spent about $493 million. Almost half of the tourists are from El Salvador and the United States.

Weights and Measures

Guatemala uses a mixture of American, metric, and old Spanish weights and measures.

Weights are in pounds and ounces. Cloth is measured in yards, but not feet and inches. Kilometers are used for road distances, and meters for houses.

Land, on the other hand, is measured in *varas*, a length of about 33 inches (84 cm). It is also measured in *manzanas*, which equals 1.73 acres (0.7 hectares). Milk is sold in both gallons and liters, but not in pints. A *garrafon* is 5 gallons.

Tikal

Guatemala's biggest tourist attraction is Tikal, the ancient Maya city in the Petén rain forest. At the heart of the ruins is the Great Plaza. On one side is the magnificent Temple of the Jaguar, a 144-foot-high (44-m), steep-sided pyramid. It was built as a tomb for Ah Cacaw, who became ruler of Tikal in the year 682. The Temple of Masks stands on the opposite side of the plaza. Occupying the whole north side of the plaza is the North Acropolis, which includes twelve temples. On the south side is the Central Acropolis, a maze of tiny rooms and stairways built around courtyards. Beyond the Great Plaza, there are many more temples, pyramids, plazas, and houses to explore. Visitors who stay the night will get to hear the sounds of the jungle. Dawn and dusk are alive with the screeching of toucans and parakeets.

What a Quetzal Can Buy in the Market

Item	Cost in Quetzals	Cost in U.S. Dollars
1 pound (0.5 kg) of rice	Q2.75	$0.38
1 pound (0.5 kg) of black beans	Q3.00	$0.39
5 pounds (2.2 kg) of sugar	Q8.50	$1.10
I pound (0.5 kg) of ground coffee	Q23.00	$2.99
100 juice oranges	Q25.00	$3.25
Large toothpaste	Q9.00	$1.17
Can of Coca-Cola	Q3.50	$.45
6 corn tortillas	Q1.00	$.13
80 pieces of firewood	Q45.00	$5.84
Boy's school shoes	Q170.00	$22.08

Transportation

Guatemala has over 8,500 miles (14,000 km) of road. Less than a third are paved. The principal highway runs from Chiapas, Mexico, to Guatemala City and then south into El Salvador. Guatemala City is also connected to Belize City and to the Caribbean and Pacific coasts by good highways. Small roads branch off the highways into the highlands, but the roads are poor in many areas. Villagers in remote places often have to walk many miles to reach the nearest good road.

Guatemalan villagers on a rural road

Railroads in Guatemala have been in decline for many years. Today, the country has no passenger service. Some sections of freight railroad are now being updated. Guatemala's main ports are Puerto Barrios and Santo Tomás de Castilla on the Caribbean coast and Champerico on the Pacific coast.

Newspapers with headlines on the Guatemalan elections

Communications

Most of the news media in Guatemala are owned by private businesses that support the country's government. Guatemala officially recognizes freedom of the press in its constitution. Newspapers do criticize government policies, but journalists, especially those exposing corruption, are often threatened. The main newspapers are *Prensa Libre*, *Siglo Veintiuno*, *La Hora*, and *El Periodico*.

There are five government, six educational, and ninety-one commercial radio broadcasting services in Guatemala. Because radio reaches the most remote parts of the country, it is the way most people get their news. The nation also has twenty-six television stations.

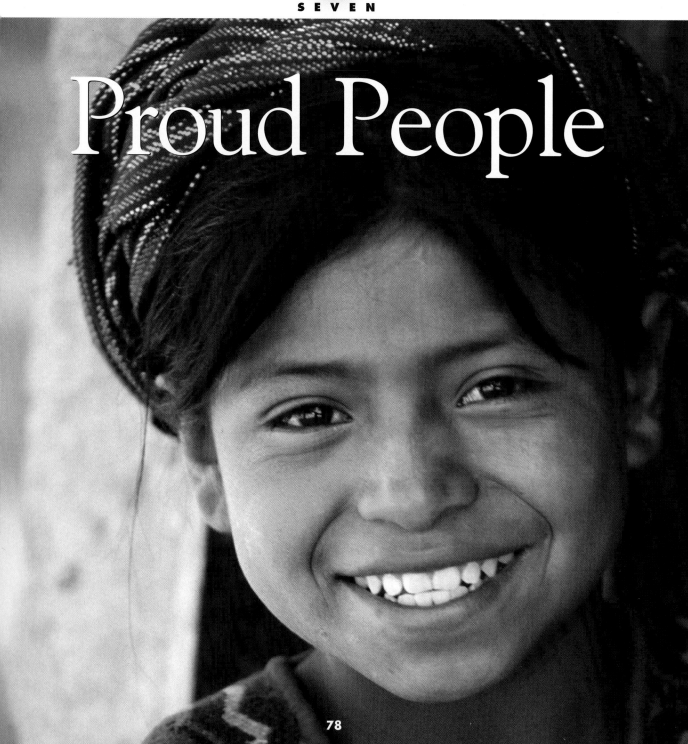

Proud People

78

ABOUT FOURTEEN MILLION PEOPLE LIVE IN GUATEMALA. The nation's population is young, with 43 percent of the people under age fourteen. Guatemala's population is roughly divided between native people—mostly Maya—and ladinos, people who have mixed Spanish and native parentage. In Guatemala, there are twenty different native groups descended from the Maya and one non-Maya group, the Xinca, who live in the southeast. The native people speak their own languages, though many also speak Spanish. The ladinos speak Spanish. A small number of Garifuna, people of African descent, live on the Caribbean coast. White Guatemalans of European descent are very few in number but hold most of the political and economic power in the country.

Opposite: **A large percentage of Guatemala's population consists of young people.**

An older Guatemalan man and a young girl

Who Lives in Guatemala?

Ladinos	55%
Native people	43%
Whites and others	2%

A young Cakchiquel Indian girl stands next to hand-woven fabrics.

It is often difficult to tell the difference between ladinos and native people. In some cases, people are considered Maya if they wear traditional dress and speak a native language. Native people can sometimes appear to be ladinos simply by a change of dress and by speaking Spanish.

Ladinos tend to live in Guatemala City and other cities and towns. A few ladinos are members of the wealthy and powerful elite. But most are middle class or working class. They are poorer than most people in North America or Europe, but they live, dress, and work in much the same way.

Maya girls posing in a city plaza

The Maya

The Maya people of Guatemala are broken into twenty different groups. The largest native groups are the Mam, who live in the west; the Quiché, to the north and west of Lake Atitlán; the Cakchiquel, between the eastern shores of Lake Atitlán and Guatemala City; and the Kekchi, in the mountains to the north and west of Lake Izabal. Other groups include the Pokomam, Tzutujil, Achi, and Chortí.

Some rural areas are inhabited solely by the Maya. In recent times, more people have moved from rural areas to cities seeking work and better education and health care.

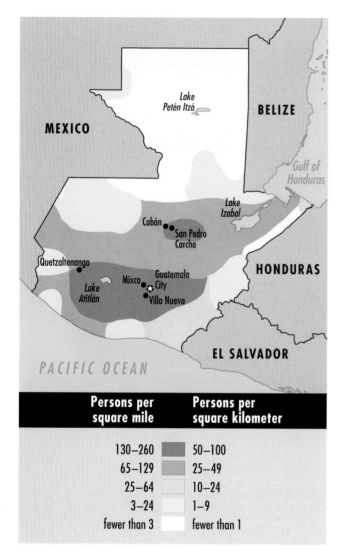

Persons per square mile		Persons per square kilometer	
130–260		50–100	
65–129		25–49	
25–64		10–24	
3–24		1–9	
fewer than 3		fewer than 1	

The Maya have been abused and exploited since colonial times, first by wealthy landowners and then by the ladinos. Throughout the years, the government has failed to provide them education, medical care, or land. During the civil war, they received particularly brutal treatment by the army and Civil Defense Patrols.

Despite the discrimination, the Maya have clung firmly to their traditions and culture. Among the most vibrant expressions of their culture are the brilliantly colored weavings. These are decorated with centuries-old designs that relate to their myths and religion. The best places to see these weavings are in busy, crowded markets in the western highlands. Markets are essential to the Maya way of life. People walk many miles, sometimes carrying produce on their backs, to trade with their neighbors and sell weavings to tourists. Markets also serve as important gathering places for families scattered over the remote hillsides.

Maya communities and villages have always looked after their own affairs and protected their traditions and culture.

They do not welcome outsiders. Authority lies with a Council of Elders who discuss village matters, make judgments, and pass laws. A group of men known as the *cofradia* is responsible for looking after the village patron saint and arranging festivals in his or her honor. Spiritual guides minister to those in need and use herbal medicine to help the sick. They are also the keepers of the Maya calendar and give advice on the best days to hold festivals or bring in the harvest. Villages have a mayor who serves for a year and is the official representative of the community to the outside world.

Since the late 1980s, the Maya have formed organizations to fight for better treatment. One mark of their progress is that the government now recognizes that native languages should be legal and taught in schools.

Populations of Major Guatemalan Cities (2005 estimate)

Guatemala City	964,823
Mixco	297,039
Villa Nueva	218,294
Quetzaltenango	112,121
Escuintla	69,311

Maya priests pray during the New Year's celebration.

Garifuna

The Garifuna live along a short stretch of the Caribbean coast. They are descended from African slaves who escaped to the West Indian island of Saint Vincent and mixed with the

A Garifuna family in Livingston

local Carib people. In 1795, they staged a rebellion against their British rulers. They escaped to an island off of Honduras. From there, they spread out along the mainland. In Guatemala, the main Garifuna settlement is the small town of Livingston, which is home to about 4,000 people. Each November, Livingston holds a festival with traditional music and dancing to celebrate the arrival of the first Garifuna on Guatemalan soil.

Small numbers of blacks also live in the nearby ports of Puerto Barrios and Santo Tomas. They are descended from people brought from Jamaica by the United Fruit Company to work on the banana plantations.

Guatemala's Languages

Spanish is Guatemala's official language and the primary language of 60 percent of the population. Twenty-three Maya languages have survived. Cakchiquel, Kekchí, Mam, and Quiché are the most widely spoken. The Garifuna have their own language, but only a few people speak it. English is widely understood among the upper class, businesspeople, and some Garifuna.

Major Mayan Languages of Guatemala

- Mayan language area
- Garifuna language area
- Non-Mayan language area
- *Pokomam* Mayan language

Speaking Spanish

The Spanish alphabet has 28 letters. It does not have *k* or *w*, but does include the letters *ch*, *ll*, *ñ*, and *rr*. Spanish vowels have a single sound and are always pronounced the same way:

a   as in father

e   as in met

i   as in seek

o   as in toe

u   as in rude

Consonants are similar to those in English but with some exceptions:

b and *v* sound the same

d within a word is pronounced th—except after *l* and *n*, when it is pronounced like the *d* in desk

h is not pronounced

j has no exact equivalent in English, but is like an *h* in happy

ll is similar to *y* in yacht

ñ as in onion

qu replaces the k sound

rr is strongly rolled

A Few Words in Quiché

I	*yin*
We	*uj*
One	*jun*
Two	*queb*
Woman	*ixok*
Person	*winak*
Man	*achi*
Bird	*tz'iquin*
Dog	*tz'l*
Tree	*che'*
Leaf	*uxak*
Fish	*car*

The Role of Women

Guatemala's constitution states that men and women have equal rights, but in practice men are head of the household and family. A woman is expected to care for the family and obey her husband. A law passed in 1996 protects women from violence in the home, but domestic abuse remains a problem. It is estimated that about a third of Guatemalan women are abused. Hundreds of women are murdered by their husbands every year.

Women are less likely to go to school than men, so many more women than men are unable to read and write. In some

Rosalina Tuyuc (left)

Maya areas, only 1 percent of women go beyond elementary school, and over 85 percent cannot read or write.

Women make up about one-fifth of the country's workforce and almost 40 percent of the workers in Guatemala City. Many are employed in factories, where they typically work a twelve-hour day for less than six dollars. Since the 1990s, an increasing number of organizations have been founded across the country to help women.

Few women have made it to the top of their professions. But some have made their mark. Congresswomen Nineth Montenegro and Nobel Prize winner Rigoberta Menchú Tum are at the forefront of the fight for human rights. Rosalina Tuyuc was the first Maya congresswoman. More recently, she has served as the director of the National Reparation Program for the Victims of the Armed Conflict.

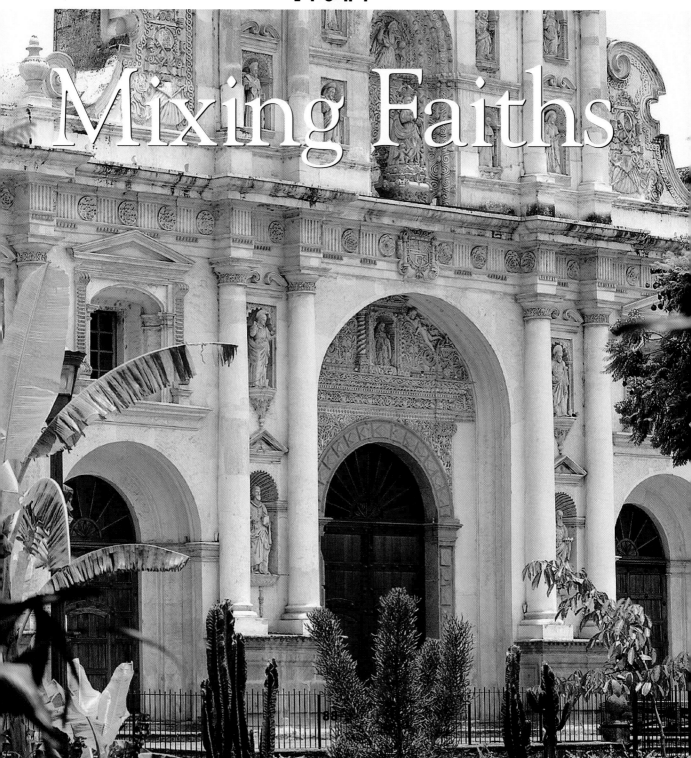

Mixing Faiths

Maya Indian priestesses

Roman Catholicism has been the dominant religion in Guatemala since the arrival of the Spaniards in the sixteenth century. Today, it is estimated that between 50 and 60 percent of Guatemalans are Catholic. About 40 percent are Protestant. But it is also believed that about half the population continue to practice their traditional religions, either separately or combined with Catholic beliefs. The Maya people have a deep-rooted belief in spirits, both good and evil, existing in the natural world around them. Spirit places include rocks, springs, streams, and even trees or wild animals.

Opposite: **One of Guatemala's Roman Catholic cathedrals**

A fruit and vegetable market in Chichicastenango

A Mix of Beliefs

The small town of Chichicastenango has been the home of the Quiché people for centuries. On Sundays, many Quiché from the countryside come to the town to trade in the market. They also gather at the church of Santo Tomás, or Saint Thomas. Built in 1540, the church stands on a low mound that was a sacred place before the Spaniards arrived. A flight of steps lead up to the church from the town plaza. On Sundays, a Catholic mass is held there. Many candles are lit, and the church is filled with sweet-smelling smoke from burning incense.

Religious Holidays in Guatemala

January 6	Epiphany
March or April	Holy Week
August 15	Assumption Day
November 1	All Saints' Day
December 7	Burning the Devil
December 8	Feast of the Immaculate Conception
December 25	Christmas Day

Popul Vuh

Ancient Maya beliefs were passed down from family to family by word of mouth until the mid-1500s. At that time, a group of Quiché leaders wrote the sacred book of the Maya, *Popul Vuh*, on bark paper using the Spanish alphabet.

It was not until two centuries later that a priest found the book and made a Spanish translation. The original Quiché book has been lost, but the priest's translation is in the Newberry Library in Chicago. *Popul Vuh* has been translated literally as the "book of the mat," since mats were symbols of authority in Maya society.

Some Quiché also go to the top of a nearby wooded hill. There they make offerings of flowers and food to an ancient Maya spirit, Pascual Abaj. They believe the spirit will help them with many problems of life, from troubles in marriage to improving the harvest. At the sacred site, the spirit is represented by a carved stone face set on a mound. It is surrounded by stones, small fires for burning offerings, smoke, and candles. The rituals are attended by Quiché priests and priestesses.

A woman takes part in a Guatemalan religious ritual.

Festivals

Many festivals in Guatemala are a mixture of Maya beliefs and Catholicism. In most places, villages mark the feast day of their patron saint. On this day, the villages celebrate the holy person who they believe protects their village. The villagers dress in their finest clothes and enjoy plenty of food and drink, dances, and firecrackers.

In a few places, they perform the dance of the *Palo Volador*, or "flying pole." A tall pole is erected in front of the church,

Maya people taking part in a mass

and small offerings are made for the safety of the "dancers." At the top of the pole is a rotating frame. Two or four men climb the pole. They each wind a rope around it near the top. Holding a rope, they leap into space. As the frame rotates, they spin around, falling headfirst toward the ground. The effect is spectacular. The locals say that if one of the men has committed a sin, he will crash and be killed.

Two dancers perform the dance of the Palo Volador.

Easter celebrations in
Antigua Guatemala

Holy Week, which leads up to Easter Sunday, is marked by processions and deep devotion. In many parts of the country, pageants are put on portraying the journey of Christ to the cross, where he will die. In Antigua Guatemala, thousands gather to see actors walking on elaborate carpets of flowers and colored sawdust, which symbolize Christ's pain and suffering.

Santiago Atitlán is one of the few places that still pay homage to Maximón, the drinking and smoking corn god. Every Easter, people wash and dress a statue of Maximón and then ply him with cigarettes and alcohol.

Burning the Devil

As Christmas approaches, the mixture of Catholic beliefs and belief in spirits becomes apparent. On December 7, Guatemalans celebrate the *Quema del Diablo*, or "burning the devil." Late in the evening, fires are lit and all kinds of rubbish are added to the flames until the smoke is thick. Children join in. Some have painted faces. Others wear paper masks that are later thrown into the fires.

Guatemalans celebrating the Quema del Diablo.

As Christmas approaches, many families put up Nativity scenes in their homes, showing Christ's birth in the manger. Christmas Eve is a day of festive celebration. Music pours into the streets, and as midnight nears, church bells ring. At twelve o'clock, firecrackers are set off. Christmas Day is quieter, as families gather to eat special meals. The favorite food this day is red tamales, cornhusks filled with meat and cornmeal.

Red tamales

The Black Christ

Esquipulas is a small town close to the border with El Salvador. In a huge church in Esquipulas hangs a statue of Christ on the cross. It is known as the Black Christ because of the dark brown color of the wood. In 1737, an archbishop was said to have been cured of an illness by the miraculous powers of the carving. Since then, the Black Christ has become the greatest pilgrimage site in Central America. Each year, hundreds of thousands of pilgrims visit the town to pay homage to the carving and seek its help.

Evangelism

These many festivals have long been part of Guatemalan tradition in the regions where Maya and ladino cultures are dominant. But there have been attempts to change it. During Guatemala's brutal military regimes, the Maya were sometimes forced to practice their rituals in secret. At the same time, North American Protestant evangelical churches were given free rein to move into the communities. Evangelical churches actively try to convert people to their beliefs, and conflict between various religions arose.

The evangelical churches have spread to many remote parts of Guatemala, and their number of followers is increasing. Their appeal lies partly in work they have done in poor areas. Evangelicals have built schools and health clinics and run food programs. They also appeal to the Maya because they broadcast by radio in some native languages. Many people are drawn to evangelistic churches because these churches oppose drinking and gambling and seem to offer the hope of a more stable life. Among the evangelical groups active in Guatemala are Jehovah's Witnesses, the Assembly of God, the Church of Latter-Day Saints, and the Prince of Peace Church.

Other Faiths

Guatemala is also home to small numbers of people who follow other religions. The Garifuna of the Caribbean coast follow a mixture of African, native, and Catholic religions. Each May, the Garifuna in Livingston celebrate the festival of San Isidro Labrador. The festival includes dancing the hunga-hunga, a religious dance that is supposed to enable the living to communicate with the dead.

Guatemala is also home to about 1,200 Jews and an equally small number of Muslims. Most live in Guatemala City. The Baha'i faith has a following of 20,000, and there are scattered groups of Mennonites.

Native Quiche people praying
at an evangelical meeting

Vibrant Culture

G UATEMALA HAS A RICH CULTURAL HERITAGE. THE MAYA are a great part of that. People today still marvel at their artifacts and ruins from a thousand years ago. But the Maya are also vibrant living communities. They have preserved their languages and traditional crafts and festivals. Guatemalan artists and writers draw heavily on Maya culture and tradition.

Opposite: **A marimba player in Antigua Guatemala**

Popul Vuh Museum

The Popul Vuh Museum in Guatemala City takes its name from the sacred book of the Quiché. The museum houses ancient artifacts, exhibits about Mayan folklore, and colonial art.

The first room contains one of the world's best displays of burial urns (left). Some of the urns are large enough to have held an actual dead body. Others contained a person's precious belongings. Some of the urns have wild decorations. Some have skulls. Others have grotesque faces. Still others show animals such as the jaguar. The museum also houses displays of ceramic bowls, vases, plates, and other artifacts. The oldest ceramics date back to 50 B.C. A collection of stone yokes thought to have been used by players of the Maya ballgame are also on exhibit.

Guatemala's political history greatly affected its writers. Many works by Guatemalan writers have not been published because of government censorship. A lot of writers were forced to leave the country for Mexico, Europe, or the United States. Guatemala's greatest writer, Miguel Angel Asturias, was one of those who had to leave the country. He won the Nobel Prize for Literature.

Miguel Angel Asturias

In 1967, Miguel Angel Asturias became the first Latin American writer to win the Nobel Prize for Literature. Asturias was born in Guatemala City in 1899. He grew up during the regime of the dictator Manuel Estrada Cabrera. In 1923, he graduated from the University of San Carlos. Following that, he studied anthropology and Maya languages in Paris, France.

In 1930, he published *Legends of Guatemala*, which won an award for the best Spanish-American book published in France. His first novel was *The President*. This story reflects the corrupt and evil world under the Cabrera dictatorship. The book went unpublished for thirteen years until Juan José Arévalo became president in 1944 and allowed more freedom and openness.

In the 1940s, Asturias produced what many believe is his masterpiece, *Men of Maize*. It is a story of rebellion by a remote native group that is then slaughtered by the army. It is written as a myth, drawing on the magic world of the native peoples. Asturias is also known for his so-called Banana Trilogy. These three novels criticize the United Fruit Company and the effect of North American involvement in the Guatemalan economy. Asturias also wrote poems, plays, and short stories.

Among the best known of today's writers is Arturo Arias (1950–), whose work *After the Bombs* reflects the views of a young boy living in Guatemala City during a period of military coups. In his book *The Bird Who Cleans the World and Other Mayan Fables*, Victor Montejo (1951–) relates Maya myths and fables told to him by his mother, and he draws parallels with today's social and political problems. Francisco Goldman (1954–) won an award for *The Long Night of White Chickens*, a story set in Guatemala City during the worst of the killings.

Testimonials are a form of contemporary Guatemalan literature that relate the true, personal experiences of the native people. The most famous is *I, Rigoberta Menchú*, which was first published in 1983. Among others are *Son of Tecún Umán: A Maya Indian Tells His Life Story* by Ignacio Bizarro Uj-Pan and *Days of the Jungle: The Testimony of a Guatemalan Guerrillero*, 1972–1976 by Mario Payeras.

Carlos Merida

Artists

Many Guatemalan artists have also been inspired by the lives of Guatemala's native people and Maya history. Carlos Merida (1891–1984) is thought by many to be the father of modern art in Guatemala. He spent

Opposite: **A painting by Juan Sisay**

much of his life in Mexico. His works include murals painted in Mexico and Guatemala, and a glass mosaic in Guatemala's Municipal Palace. Alfredo Gálvez Suárez (1899–1946) and Antonio Tejeda Fonseca (1908–1966) painted landscapes and romanticized the lives of the native peoples. Roberto Gonzalez Goyri (1924–) is a leading Guatemalan sculptor who late in life became a painter. He worked with Merida and others to create mosaic and carved murals in Guatemala City's Civic Centre.

Artists continue to highlight the difficulties faced by the Maya. Manolo Gallardo (1936–) paints portraits of the Quiché, highlighting their plight. Printmaker and painter Moises Barrios (1946–) focuses on ordinary people and the reality of the world in which they live.

A group of Maya artists from San Juan Comalapa, Santiago Atitlán, and San Pedro la Laguna have achieved international acclaim with their painting. These artists, who mostly paint with oils, are untrained. They depict local scenes, landscapes, and people. Juan Sisay, the first oil painter in Santiago Atitlán, began painting around 1950. He achieved early success but was assassinated in 1989. His brother, two sons, and grandson are all painters. In the village of San Pedro on the north side of Lake Atitlán, Rafael González y González in 1929 first mixed dyes used for fabric with the sap of a local tree in order to paint. His grandson, Pedro Rafael Gonzalez Chavajay, was the first oil painter in San Pedro. He and his cousin Mariano Gonzalez, are considered San Pedro's finest artists.

Day of the Dead

November 1, the Day of the Dead, is when Guatemalans remember those who have died. They spend time in the cemetery, placing lilies and marigold petals on the graves. In the Cakchiquel village of Santiago Sacatepeques, the custom is to fly kites. These are not just ordinary kites; they're huge, some 20 feet (6 m) across. The kites are a symbolic link between the living and the dead. They are supposed to rid the cemetery of evil spirits. Each kite has a huge bamboo frame. Layers of colored tissue paper are then worked into intricate patterns to make the kite. Several people are needed to get the kites off the ground.

Handicrafts

Guatemala produces some of the finest textiles in Latin America. The mix of rich, vibrant colors and highly intricate embroidered designs is unique. The Maya mostly use two types of loom, the backstrap and foot looms. Most clothing is woven on small, portable backstrap looms. The weaver attaches one end of the loom to a post or tree, and the other end around the waist, so that by leaning back she can control the tension on the weaving. The foot, or treadle, loom was introduced by the Spaniards. They are large and generally worked by men.

A Guatemalan woman using a loom to weave colorful cloth

Designs embroidered on textiles include birds and animals, plants and flowers, doll-like human figures, and geometric shapes. The most common birds are hens, peacocks, eagles, quetzals, and turkeys, as well as a double-headed bird. Deer, monkeys, and other animals significant to Maya lore are also common. The most widely used designs are geometric shapes. Some of these are symbolic, such as a zigzag line that is thought to represent the god of lightning. Each village has its own designs, patterns, and colors.

A Guatemalan shirt embroidered with a flower design

Other Maya crafts include bags made from the fibers of the agave plant, brightly painted wood carvings of animals and birds, wooden masks, bamboo baskets, mats, and jewelry in silver, jade, and other semiprecious stones.

Textile products at a Guatemalan market stall

Folk Dances

Guatemalans have many folk dances that relate to their history. Some go back to the time the Spaniards first arrived. Others go back far beyond that. Each dance has its own intricate costumes, and many involve human or animal masks.

Some dances tell a story, such as the Dance of the Conquest, which portrays Pedro de Alvarado defeating Tecún Umán. The Deer Dance is common in most parts of Guatemala. It dates back to an ancient Maya hunting ceremony.

Music

Guatemalan music has Spanish, Mayan, and Garifuna origins. Today, it is also influenced by North American and European pop music. Guatemala's basic traditional instrument is the marimba. It is similar to a xylophone, but it is bigger and is played by several musicians at the same time. The sounds of the marimba are heard at every fiesta and celebration. In the cities, marimba orchestras perform at important events and celebrations. These bands also includes trumpets, saxophones,

Marimba players

banjos, and percussion instruments. Probably the best-known marimba song is the waltz "Luna de Xelaju," which was composed in 1942 by Paco Pérez.

Garifuna music is based on different types of drums, but also includes shakers, scrapers, and other percussion instruments. Modern ladino music is a mixture of Western pop, Latin rhythms such as cumbia, salsa, and meringue, and mariachi music.

Sports

Guatemalans love sports. Soccer is the most popular sport, followed by baseball and basketball. Bicycle races are major events, with tours in many towns and cities. In October and December, bullfights draw large crowds in Guatemala City. The bullfighters are not usually Guatemalan, however; they are Spanish or Mexican.

The Little Fish

Nicknamed *Pescadito*, or "little fish," Carlos Ruiz is one of the best soccer players to come out of Guatemala. He currently plays for the Los Angeles Galaxy, in the United States. Ruiz was born in 1979 and began playing professional soccer at age sixteen. He made his debut on the Guatemalan national team in 1998 during a benefit match for the victims of Hurricane Mitch. He signed up with the Los Angeles team in 2002 and was an immediate success, scoring twenty-five goals in his first season. That year, he also won the league's Most Valuable Player award.

Mario Acevedo (left) with
Angel Sanabria

Everyday Life

HOW PEOPLE LIVE IN GUATEMALA DEPENDS A GREAT deal on their ethnicity. Almost all wealthy people are of Spanish background. The Maya, on the other hand, have poverty rates that may reach as high as 90 percent.

Opposite: **A young Indian boy carrying wood**

Rural Life

Most Maya live in the western highlands in small towns and villages scattered over the hillsides. Their daily work is farming a plot of land called the *milpa*, where they grow corn,

A rooster scavenges near a family's home in rural Guatemala.

beans, squash, chiles, and other crops. The milpa can be several hours from the farmer's home. He will rise early and return home by dusk. Peasant farmers work using a wooden hoe and a digging stick. Milpas are sometimes on hillsides so steep that the farmer must tie himself to a tree stump or boulder while tilling the ground. Maya families also raise chickens, ducks, pigs, sheep, and goats.

Maya custom is for fathers to divide their plot of land between sons, so the plots have become smaller. They are so small, in fact, that many people cannot feed their families with what they grow on their land. Also, much of the good land has been taken for growing coffee and other export crops. Some Maya have been forced to grow nontraditional crops such as broccoli and strawberries to earn money. Others survive by working on banana and sugar plantations on the coast for several months each year.

Military service attracts some Maya, while others have migrated to cities and towns. There the Maya and poor ladinos are at the lowest level of society. Untrained and unskilled, few jobs are open to them. Sometimes they can find work cleaning houses or shining shoes, but most become street traders, selling anything from textiles to trinkets. Nowhere is the divide between the wealthy elite and the poor as obvious as in Guatemala City, which has both orphan children begging on the streets and huge mansions for the wealthy.

National Holidays

January 1	New Year's Day
January 6	Epiphany
March or April	Easter Week (Holy Week)
May 1	Labor Day
June 30	Army Day
August 15	Feast of the Assumption (Assumption Day)
September 15	Independence Day
October 12	Discovery of America
October 20	Revolution Day
November 1	All Saints' Day
December 24–25	Christmas
December 31	New Year's Eve

Housing

A traditional rural Maya home is built of adobe mud brick or cornstalks. It has a tiled or thatched roof. Today, people often use concrete blocks and corrugated iron roofing. A simple house has just one room, with a table and chairs or stools, roughly constructed beds, and a pile of stones to form a stove. Better-off Maya homes have a separate kitchen. A few still have an outdoor steam-bath hut, called a *temaxcal*. Inside the hut, bathers light a fire to heat the stones. They then throw water on the stones to produce steam. These huts have been around since ancient times.

Maya houses in Chichicastenango

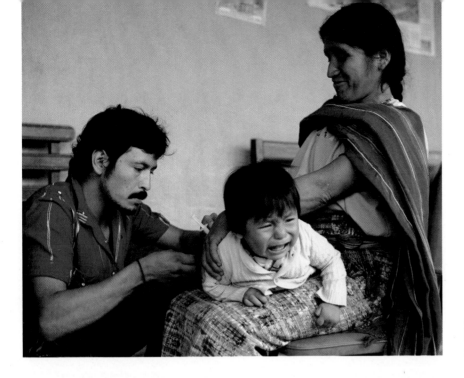

A Guatemalan Indian woman holds her baby while he receives a vaccination.

Housing in urban areas is much the same as in the United States and Europe. Housing ranges from high-rise apartment buildings to small concrete houses. The wealthy often live in large houses surrounded by well-kept lawns.

Health

Most doctors work in Guatemala City. Health clinics in rural areas are more likely to be staffed by nurses and doctors-in-training. Only about half the population has access to health care. For medical treatment, the Maya often go first to their *zahorin*, the traditional healer, who uses charms, herbs, and prayers to try to cure illnesses. Guatemalans suffer from one of the highest infant mortality rates in Central America with 37 deaths per 1,000 live births. On average, Guatemalans live just sixty-five years, compared with seventy-seven years in the United States.

Education

Elementary education is free and compulsory for children between seven and fourteen years of age. Secondary education starts at age thirteen and lasts up to six years. Though everyone is supposed to attend elementary school, in fact many children do not. School enrollment in rural areas is much lower than in cities because of a lack of schools. Many rural schools only go to third grade. Maya girls are the least likely to attend school. Guatemala has one of the lowest rates of literacy in Central America, with only about 71 percent of people over the age of fifteen able to read and write. The percentage is much lower in rural areas than in urban areas.

Public schools are badly funded. Buildings are often in poor condition, without a roof or windows. The children frequently have to sit on blocks and write on their laps. Equipment is in short supply, and in rural areas especially there is often a poor level of teaching.

At most schools, children wear a uniform. For the boys, it is white short-sleeved shirts and long gray pants. For the girls, it is checked skirts, white blouses, and tall socks. Maya children wear traditional dress. In addition to public schools, some churches, both Catholic and Protestant, run schools. They can be expensive, but the standard of teaching is higher than in public schools. Because of this, even poor people try to send their children to these schools.

The country's oldest university, San Carlos, was founded in 1676. Tuition is free, but the university has long been underfunded. It has also suffered from decades of political turmoil.

Private universities include Rafael Landívar, Mariano Gálvez, the University of Del Valle, and Francisco Marroquín University. All are in Guatemala City, although some have branches in other cities.

These children learn in a simple classroom with a soil floor.

A Maya woman preparing tortillas

Food

Corn and black beans are the staples of Maya cooking. Corn is used to make tortillas, which are cooked on a *comale*, a sheet of metal placed over a fire. Tortillas are sometimes eaten with pieces of meat or chiles. Corn is also used in snacks such as tamales (cornmeal stuffed with chicken and cooked in corn-husks). Beans are boiled, mashed, and refried or cooked with

Fiambre

Fiambre is eaten on the Day of the Dead. It is a huge dish of cold meats, fish, and vegetables. The meats include tongue, chicken, pork, beef, ham, and sausages. The fish are most likely sardines or mackerel. Vegetables used may include carrots, potatoes, string beans, beets, peas, cabbage, and cauliflower. They are cooked, cut into small pieces, and marinated in a sauce overnight.

The sauce is made from parsley, green onions, mustard seed, chiles, ginger, dry mustard, salt, oil, and vinegar. Just before serving, the meats and vegetables are mixed together with a few capers. They are then arranged on lettuce leaves. Olives, pieces of cheese, peppers, onions, sliced hard-boiled eggs, parsley, and anchovies are added as decoration. Finally, grated cheese is sprinkled on top. This feast is served with rolls and tortillas.

onion and served whole. They are often the only source of protein Maya families have, and they are eaten with virtually every meal. Stews made with beef, chicken, turkey, or duck are another popular dish, particularly in cold highland areas.

A basket of black beans

Ladinos eat the same food as the Maya, but they have other choices as well. In urban areas, American fast-food, pizza, pasta, and Chinese food are popular. Markets in cities are also well-stocked with fruits and vegetables, and dairy products are readily available. Food on the Caribbean coast is quite different from that of the highlands. There, bananas, coconuts, and seafood are the basis of most dishes.

Maya Dress

Maya women's traditional clothing is called *traje*. Much of it is woven by hand. The traditional clothing consists of the *huipil*, or blouse, a skirt, a sash, a hair ribbon, a shawl, and a piece of cloth called a *tzute*. The designs and colors differ from village to village, as do the hairstyle and the way the belt and skirt are worn. Children's dress is similar to those of the parents.

The huipil is made of two or three woven lengths of cloth sewn together to make a square. It is decorated with embroidered designs. The square is folded in half, and a hole is cut in the center where the head goes through. Sometimes the sides are sewed together, leaving armholes at the top. Other times they are left open. There are two types of skirts. One is a simple wraparound skirt. The other is a skirt gathered at the waist. In both cases, dark blue is a traditional color. Sashes are usually wound around the waist several times.

Hair ribbons vary from simple everyday bands to 25-foot-long (8-m) ribbons for special occasions. The women of Santiago Atitlán sometimes wear a narrow ribbon 40 feet

A market seller in Chichicastenango wearing a brightly colored shirt and pants held in place by a sash

(12 m) long. Women use tzutes for carrying babies or produce, or as a head covering in the sun.

Most Maya men prefer Western clothing. Traditional dress consists of a shirt, which can be plain or ornately embroidered, and trousers, which sometimes have brightly colored stripes or geometric or animal designs. Pants are held in place by a sash that is tied in different ways according to the village custom. Many men continue to wear sashes long after they have switched to Western dress. Men also sometimes wear *ponchitos*, a woolen blanket worn over the trousers.

The Future

Guatemala and its people have lived through troubled times. Though the Peace Accords marked the beginning of a new chapter for the country, many problems remain. Despite the nation's long history of violence, the Guatemalan people remain a remarkably friendly lot. In bustling markets, on crowded buses, or on quiet mountaintops, visitors will always find a welcoming face and a helping hand.

Both Guatemalan military officials (left) and civilians continue to work toward a more peaceful nation.

Timeline

Guatemalan History		World History
		2500 B.C. Egyptians build the Pyramids and the Sphinx in Giza.
Ancestors of the Maya begin living in villages.	1000 B.C.	
		563 B.C. The Buddha is born in India.
Maya civilization reaches its peak.	A.D. 250–900	A.D. **313** The Roman emperor Constantine recognizes Christianity.
		610 The Prophet Muhammad begins preaching a new religion called Islam.
Maya civilization declines.	900s	**1054** The Eastern (Orthodox) and Western (Roman) Churches break apart.
		1066 William the Conqueror defeats the English in the Battle of Hastings.
		1095 Pope Urban II proclaims the First Crusade.
		1215 King John seals the Magna Carta.
		1300s The Renaissance begins in Italy.
		1347 The Black Death sweeps through Europe.
		1453 Ottoman Turks capture Constantinople, conquering the Byzantine Empire.
		1492 Columbus arrives in North America.
The Spanish conquest of Guatemala begins.	1523	**1500s** The Reformation leads to the birth of Protestantism.
Santiago de los Caballeros de Guatemala is founded as the capital.	1542	
Guatemala City becomes the capital.	1776	**1776** The Declaration of Independence is signed.
		1789 The French Revolution begins.
Guatemala declares itself independent from Spain.	1821	
Guatemala joins the United Provinces of Central America.	1823	
The United Provinces of Central America splits into separate countries.	1840	

Guatemalan History		World History	
José Rafael Carrera becomes the first president of Guatemala.	1844		
		1865	The American Civil War ends.
Guatemala's coffee boom begins.	1870		
The United Fruit Company is founded.	1899		
Manuel Estrada Cabrera begins his twenty-two-year rule as dictator.	1898		
The Santa María volcano erupts violently.	1902		
		1914	World War I breaks out.
		1917	The Bolshevik Revolution brings communism to Russia.
		1929	Worldwide economic depression begins.
		1939	World War II begins, following the German invasion of Poland.
Juan José Arévalo becomes president in democratic elections.	1945	1945	World War II ends.
President Jacobo Arbenz Guzman enacts a law giving land to poor families.	1952		
Arbenz is forced from office.	1954		
		1957	The Vietnam War starts.
Guatemala's first guerrilla movement is formed.	1960		
Miguel Angel Asturias wins the Nobel Prize for Literature.	1967		
		1969	Humans land on the moon.
		1975	The Vietnam War ends.
An earthquake kills 23,000 people in Guatemala.	1976		
General Benedicto Lucas Garcia becomes president; civil war violence increases.	1978		
		1979	Soviet Union invades Afghanistan.
		1983	Drought and famine in Africa.
Vinicio Cerezo Arévalo is elected the first civilian president in twenty years.	1985		
		1989	The Berlin Wall is torn down, as communism crumbles in Eastern Europe.
		1991	Soviet Union breaks into separate states.
Rigoberta Menchú Tum receives the Nobel Peace Prize.	1992	1992	Bill Clinton is elected U.S. president.
The Peace Accords are signed, ending thirty-six years of civil war.	1996		
		2000	George W. Bush is elected U.S. president.
		2001	Terrorists attack World Trade Towers, New York and the Pentagon, Washington, D.C.

Fast Facts

Official name: Republic of Guatemala

Capital: Guatemala City

Official language: Spanish

The town of Flores

Guatemala's flag

Official religion:	None
Founding date:	1847
National anthem:	"Guatemala Feliz"
Government:	Republic
Chief of state:	President
Head of government:	President
Area:	42,042 square miles (108,889 sq km)
Highest elevation:	Volcán Tajumulco 13,846 feet (4,220 m) above sea level
Lowest elevation:	Sea level along the coasts
Longest river:	Motagua, 250 miles (400 km)
Largest lake:	Izabal, 228 square miles (590 sq km)
Greatest annual precipitation:	In the Petén, up to 150 inches (380 cm)
Lowest annual precipitation:	Motagua Valley, less than 20 inches (50 cm)
National population (2004):	14,200,000

Population of largest cities (2005):

Guatemala City	964,823
Mixco	297,039
Villa Nueva	218,294
Quetzaltenango	112,121
Escuintla	69,311

The Motagua River

Ancient ruins at Tikal

Guatemalan currency

Famous landmarks:	▶ *Tikal National Park,* the Petén
	▶ *Antigua Guatemala*
	▶ *Saint Thomas Church*, Chichicastenango
	▶ *Lake Atitlán*
	▶ *Popul Vuh Museum*, Guatemala City
Industry:	Guatemala's main exports are sugar, coffee, and bananas, but in recent years the economy has diversified. The country now exports other fruits, winter vegetables, cut flowers, ornamental plants, and cardamom. Guatemala has an expanding industrial sector. The country produces processed food, textiles, plastic and paper products, and pharmaceuticals. There is also a growing number of tax-free factories owned by both Guatemalan and foreign companies, which produce mainly clothing. Guatemala has few mineral resources.
Currency:	Guatemala's currency is the quetzal. The quetzal is divided into 100 centavos; one U.S. dollar is worth 7.71 quetzals.
Weights and measures:	Guatemala uses a mixture of American, metric, and old Spanish weights and measures
Literacy rate:	71 percent

Maya girls standing in a city plaza

Rigoberta Menchú Tum

Common Spanish words and phrases:

Buenos días	Good morning
Cuánto?	How much?
Dónde está?	Where is it?
Gracias	Thank-you
Qué hora es?	What time is it?
Tengo hambre	I am hungry.

Famous Guatemalans:

Miguel Angel Asturias (1899–1974)
Winner of the Nobel Prize for Literature

Manuel Estrada Cabrera (1857–1924)
Guatemalan dictator

José Rafael Carrera (1814–1865)
Guatemala's first president

Rigoberta Menchú Tum (1959–)
Human rights activist and winner of the Nobel Peace Prize

Carlos Merida (1891–1984)
Artist

Carlos Ruiz (1979–)
Soccer player

To Find Out More

Books

▶ Dendinger, Roger E. *Guatemala*. Philadelphia: Chelsea House, 2004.

▶ Naden, Corrine J., and Rose Blue. *Ancient Maya and Tikal*. Minneapolis: Lake Street Publishers, 2003.

▶ Shea, Maureen E. *Culture and Customs of Guatemala*. Westport, Conn.: Greenwood Press, 2001.

▶ Vecciato, Gianni. *Guatemala Rainbow*. San Francisco: Pomegranate Artbooks, 1989.

Web Sites

▶ **Rabbit in the Moon: Mayan Glyphs and Architecture** www.halfmoon.org *Instructive and fun site on Mayan language, with sound and hieroglyphs.*

► CIA World Factbook 2004
http://www.cia.gov/cia/publications/
factbook/geos/gt.html
Facts and statistics on Guatemala.

Places to Contact

► **Embassy of Guatemala**
2220 R Street NW
Washington, DC 20008
(202) 745-4952

Index

Page numbers in *italics* indicate illustrations.

Meet the Author

Almost from the time Marion Morrison graduated from the University of Wales, her life has been devoted to writing about Latin America. She began with short features for British newspapers and has contributed to magazines in the United Kingdom and Peru. She has traveled widely throughout Latin America. For much of her traveling life, she has been married to Tony, whose interest in Latin America is expressed through television, photography, and writing. Together, they founded a picture library specializing in Latin America.

Marion says, "In preparation for this book, I had to rely on my past travels, as much of Guatemala has an internal security problem. Fortunately, by e-mail I can keep in touch with people living there, and this helped put a clear perspective on reports of current events." She continues, "The Internet is now an invaluable resource, and it is catching on quickly with Guatemalans, who are proud to show the world some of the

most extraordinary aspects of their country. It helps to know the ground and speak some Spanish, though even without those qualifications, the depth of information is apparent. Even small towns missed out in most books can now tell their own story. Some places have illustrations dug up from the past that would never have seen the light of day without the Web."

Marion has written other books for the Enchantment of the World series. She still travels whenever she can get a break from her desk. "I need to keep in touch," she says, "and however much I correspond or talk with other followers of Latin American studies, nothing can match a long, sometimes vigorous discussion on the spot."

Photo Credits

Alamy Images/Jamie Marshall: 24
Animals Animals/Gerard Lacz: 35
AP/Wide World Photos: 61, 84, 92
(Rodrigo Abd), 77, 113 (Moises
Castillo), 67 (Scott Dalton), 87, 89,
97 (Carlos Lopez), 110 (Jaime Puebla)
artemaya.com/Juan Sisay/Collection of
Joseph Johnston: 105
Aurora/Russell Gordon: 71
Corbis Images: 45 (Archivo Iconografico,
S.A.), 21, 131 bottom (Yann Arthus-
Bertrand), 50, 52, 102 (Bettmann),
58, 64 (Jan Butchofsky-Houser), 115
(Keith Dannemiller), 43 (Macduff
Everton), 72 (Yesica Fisch/Reuters),
55, 133 bottom (Victor Fraile/
Reuters), 19 (Arvind Garg), 119
(Bill Gentile), 15 (Jeremy Horner),
18, 123 (Dave G. Houser), 96 (Kelly-
Mooney Photography), 91 (Charles
& Josette Lenars), 29 (Buddy Mays),
83 (Ricardo Miranda/Reuters), 22
(Carl & Ann Purcell), 9 (Enzo &
Paolo Ragazzini), 26 (Galen Rowell),
95 (Jorge Silva/Reuters), 106 (Inge
Yspeert), 47, 51
Corbis Sygma/Valtierra: 127
Danita Delimont Stock Photography:
13 (Tom Boyden), 78, 125 (Judith
Haden), 34 (John & Lisa Merrill)
Getty Images: 112 (Stephen Dunn),
68 (Janeart Inc/The Image Bank),
30 (Frans Lemmens/The Image
Bank), 36 (Photodisc Blue), 53
(Frank Scherschel/Time Life
Pictures), 57 (Jorge Uzon/AFP)
National Geographic Image Collection:
41 (William Curtsinger), 37 (Roy Toft)

North Wind Picture Archives: 14
Omni-Photo Communications/
Eric Kroll: 79
Panos Pictures/Trygve Bolstad: 121
Parque Nacional Sierra del Lacandón/
Fundación Defensores de la
Naturaleza: 27, 28
Peter Arnold Inc.: 99 (Julio Etchart),
80 (Jeff Greenberg)
Photo Researchers, NY/
Jany Sauvanet: 40
photolibrary.com/William Floyd
Holdman: 76
PictureQuest/PNC/Brand X Pictures:
59, 88, 131 top
Rainbow: 107 (Dean Hulse),
108 (Coco McCoy)
Robert Fried Photography: 2, 33, 75,
81, 109, 126, 133 top
South American Pictures: 17, 116
(Robert Francis), 39 (Anna
McVittie), 7 bottom, 8, 11, 42, 101,
118, 132 top (Tony Morrison), 31,
66, 94, 111, 114, 130 (Chris Sharp)
Stone/Getty Images/James Nelson:
7 top, 90
Taxi/Getty Images/Peter Adams:
cover, 6
The Image Works: 25, 103 (Mario
Algaze), 122 (Jeff Greenberg)
TRIP Photo Library: 100 (Tibor
Bognar), 32, 93 (David Hoey),
23 (Jorge Monaco)
Woodfin Camp & Associates/Douglas
Mason: 69, 132 bottom

Maps by XNR Productions, Inc.